Porch Talk

Porch Talk

A Conversation About Archaeology in the Texas Panhandle

John R. Erickson
& Douglas K. Boyd

TEXAS TECH UNIVERSITY PRESS

This book is typeset in EB Garamond. The paper used in this book meets the minimum requirements of ANSI/NISO Z39.48-1992 (R1997). ♾

Designed by Hannah Gaskamp

Cover and interior illustrations by Nicolette G. Earley, in the style of Gerald L. Holmes

Library of Congress Cataloging-in-Publication Data

Names: Erickson, John R., 1943– author. | Boyd, Douglas K. (Douglas Kevin, 1959–) author. Title: Porch Talk: A Conversation about Archaeology in the Texas Panhandle / John R. Erickson and Douglas K. Boyd. Other titles: Conversation about Archaeology in the Texas Panhandle.

Description: Lubbock, Texas: Texas Tech University Press, 2022. | Audience: Ages 9–11 | Audience: Grades 4–6 | Summary: "A rancher and an archaeologist are curious about the ancient peoples who lived on the Texas Panhandle"— Provided by publisher.

Identifiers: LCCN 2021050013 (print) | LCCN 2021050014 (ebook) |

ISBN 978-1-68283-122-9 (paperback) | ISBN 978-1-68283-129-8 (ebook)

Subjects: LCSH: Indians of North America—Texas—Texas Panhandle—Antiquities—Juvenile literature. | Indians of North America—Great Plains—Juvenile literature. | Excavations (Archaeology)—Texas—Texas Panhandle—Juvenile literature. | Texas Panhandle (Tex.)—Antiquities—Juvenile literature.

Classification: LCC E78.T4 E75 2022 (print) | LCC E78.T4 (ebook) | DDC 976.4/8—dc23/eng/20211102

LC record available at https://lccn.loc.gov/2021050013
LC ebook record available at https://lccn.loc.gov/2021050014

Printed in the United States of America
22 23 24 25 26 27 28 29 30 / 9 8 7 6 5 4 3 2 1

Texas Tech University Press
Box 41037
Lubbock, Texas 79409-1037 USA
800.832.4042
ttup@ttu.edu
www.ttupress.org

This book is dedicated to all the people who lived on this land before us, and to all the people who want to learn more about those who came before us.

Contents

Contents

Illustrations

Illustrations

Introduction by John Erickson

Educator's Guide reference: Activity 1

I am an amateur archaeologist with no professional credentials, but I've become the custodian of a ghost town that dates to around AD 1300. It's located on my ranch in Roberts County, Texas, and it might have been occupied for fifty or a hundred years. We don't know. There's a lot we don't know.

Compared to towns of the historic era, it wasn't much—just a sprawl of widely spaced pit-houses that occupied an area of 300 acres in my West Pasture. We can only guess how many people lived there, but it was a place where babies were born and the elderly died and were buried. Women nursed children, made cornmeal in stone metates, and stitched clothes of leather while the men hunted bison with arrows tipped with points made from Alibates flint.

Maybe they sang while they worked and told stories to their children on long winter nights. Surely they spent a lot of time looking at the vastness of the starry space above them and wondered about the mystery of their existence.

This book is a conversation between me and my friend Doug Boyd, a professional archaeologist. It's the kind of conversation we might have on the porch after a day of work in the field. For more than twenty years, we have worked

Figure 1: A few of the archaeologists in the West Pasture story: John Erickson (seated in bulldozer cab), Doug Wilkens (standing left), and Doug Boyd (standing right). Photograph by Kris Erickson.

together on prehistoric sites and shared a fascination for the people who occupied them.

Our hope in writing this book is to ignite your curiosity and to make you aware of the brave and sturdy people who occupied this land long before we got here.

We'll try to strike a balance between, say, a Hank the Cowdog book that gives you laughter and entertainment and a book of scientific facts that you might find hard to read. If we spend too much time on the science, you might not read the book, but if we don't bring in some of the history of archaeology, you won't learn much.

I'm the storyteller in this venture: the landowner, the guy who walks around the ranch looking for evidence of human presence, the amateur who tries to imagine who those people were. Doug Boyd is the scientist who brings professional training and discipline to the conversation. I have learned a great deal from him, and I hope you can too.

Introduction by Douglas K. Boyd

Educator's Guide reference: Activity 1

I am a professional archaeologist with two degrees and over forty years' experience investigating archaeological sites in Texas and surrounding states. In my day job, I'm what's called a "contract archaeologist"—which is kinda like a gun for hire: "have trowel–will travel." (*Have Gun — Will Travel* was name of an old Western radio show and television series in the 1950s and 1960s. You younger folks may have to ask your parents or grandparents about this.)

In my career, I've worked in some really cool places and excavated on some fascinating prehistoric and historic sites all over Texas. None of them can compare with the coolness of the prehistoric archaeology on John Erickson's M-Cross Ranch and what we are learning about Texas Panhandle prehistory.

In this book, you'll be joining in on our discussion that will take you on a journey of archaeological discovery that has been unfolding over the last two decades. Most of these conversations took place on the front porch of the Ericksons' house, where we would sit in the evenings after a bunch of us had been digging somewhere on the ranch.

The porch is where we relaxed and socialized. The porch is where we had our best discussions about archaeology and our most profound thoughts about the people who lived on

Figure 2: Archaeologists engaged in "porch talk" on the Ericksons' front porch at the M-Cross Ranch. From left to right: Benny Roberts, Joe Rogers, Doug McGarraugh, John Erickson, Art Tawater, Tiffany Osburn, Doug Boyd, and Bill Parnell. Photograph by Doug Wilkens.

the ranch long ago. I will always treasure the memory of our many wonderful porch talks!

I got interested in archaeology when I was a kid. I was probably 9 or 10 years old when I read a book that Howard Carter (a pretty famous archaeologist) wrote about his 1922 discovery of King Tut's tomb in Egypt. The moment of discovery was thrilling, but the real story was the cataloguing, description, and analyses of all the associated artifacts.

It took them years, but what they learned about this Egyptian pharaoh was simply amazing. I was fascinated by the process of doing archaeology the right way and all the scientific methods that were involved in learning about the past. I was on my way to becoming a full-blown science nerd. I just didn't know it yet.

Our archaeological adventures on Erickson's ranch have had lots of moments of discovery, and those are amazing. But just like King Tut's tomb, each new discovery on the ranch requires lots of painstaking cataloguing, description, and analysis before we can unravel the stories about people who lived there hundreds of years ago.

Please join us in our archaeological discussion. To help you know which one of us is talking, we will preface John's remarks with **JOHN** and mine with **DOUG**.

Okay, let's get started.

Porch Talk

Chapter 1

Hobby or Science?

Educator's Guide reference: Activity 2

J OHN: I grew up in the 1950s in the little town of Perryton in the Texas Panhandle. When I was twelve, our Boy Scout troop had an overnight camp-out on a ranch near Black Mesa in northwestern Oklahoma. This was wild, empty country, and we went arrowhead hunting. The scoutmaster told us to spread out and watch the ground.

The Boy Scout motto is "Be Prepared," but we went into our relic-hunting adventure as unprepared as sheep. We supposed that arrowheads were made by Apaches, similar to those we saw in western movies. They rode horses, painted their faces, wore feathers in their hair, and attacked wagon trains. Some of them used rifles and some used bows and arrows. It never occurred to us that:

> The people who made flint tools lived on the Southern Plains somewhere between four hundred and twelve thousand years ago.
>
> They had never seen a horse or a rifle.
>
> They weren't the nineteenth-century Apaches depicted in western movies.

Chapter 1

Hollywood gave Boy Scouts some bad information about something called *archaeology*. At the age of twelve, I'm not sure I had ever heard the word or could have even spelled it. It is a big word of five syllables, derived from two Greek words that together mean "the study of ancient things."

For me, collecting arrowheads was a bit like collecting seashells on a beach. They're free. They wash up in the night, you pick them up, put them in your pocket, and take them home. I kept mine in a drawer with my socks, and there they stayed until one day, they disappeared. I never felt much curiosity about the people who made them.

I wish our scoutmaster or someone in the community had taught us some basic facts about archaeology—that it's more than collecting trinkets. It's a discipline that aims to preserve the memory of almost-forgotten people who deserve our respect.

To be fair, I must say that information about archaeology wasn't easy to find. Our little town had a few folks who collected arrowheads and displayed them in glass-covered frames, but they probably didn't know too much more about ancient cultures than I did.

Dr. Jack Hughes was a professor at West Texas State University 140 miles southwest of us. He was a smart, trained, enthusiastic, and very capable archaeologist, but I went through twelve grades in school and never heard his name.

DOUG: I was born and raised in the small farming town of Tulia. My interest in Panhandle archaeology began at the age of five or six when I started arrowhead hunting with my buddy Cody Whitten on North Tule Creek. We went down to the creek many times over a period of six or seven years. We found projectile points, scrapers, lots of flint

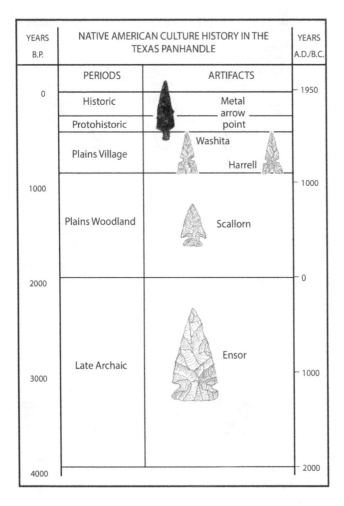

YEARS B.P.	NATIVE AMERICAN CULTURE HISTORY IN THE TEXAS PANHANDLE		YEARS A.D./B.C.
	PERIODS	ARTIFACTS	
0	Historic	Metal arrow point	1950
	Protohistoric		
	Plains Village	Washita / Harrell	
1000			1000
	Plains Woodland	Scallorn	
2000			0
3000	Late Archaic	Ensor	1000
4000			2000

Figure 3a: Arrow point chart. The Washita is the classic "style" of arrow point used by Plains Villagers in the Texas Panhandle.

flakes, and a fair amount of bone. We talked a lot about the people who might have made these things and the animals they may have hunted so long ago. In reality, we had no clue about the prehistoric people who created the artifacts that

5

Figure 3b: The Washita point in this photo is a replica made of Alibates flint and hafted to a wooden arrow shaft by a modern flint knapper. Replica arrow shaft and point made by Allen Bettis. Photograph by Doug Boyd.

we found, but that didn't matter. What did matter is that it sparked an interest in my young mind, and it made me want to learn more.

There weren't many books on archaeology in the Tulia school or public libraries, but there was an exciting book on the discovery of King Tut's tomb. It made me want to be an archaeologist. My parents encouraged my interest in the past, and they started taking me to museums. My favorite, which was close to home, was the Panhandle-Plains Historical Museum in Canyon, Texas. We would spend hours looking at the exhibits on Plains Village peoples and pioneer life in the Panhandle. I found that I was interested in everything that happened in the past.

In the winter of 1973–1974, I was lucky enough to get to work with people from West Texas State University who were doing serious, disciplined archaeology at Mackenzie Reservoir, a lake being built to supply water to Tulia and other nearby towns. I was in seventh grade and my buddy Kevin Dunn was in eighth grade. We began volunteering to work with the archaeologists every weekend, and we did this for several months (thanks to our parents who drove us back and forth!). I met and worked with many top-notch archaeologists who took us under their wings. They taught us proper archaeological field techniques as we dug at a variety of prehistoric and historic Native American sites. More importantly, they taught us how to document what we found and how to think critically about the things we saw buried in the ground.

The Lake Mackenzie experience changed my life, and archaeology became my obsession and my passion. At the age of fourteen, I decided I wanted to be a professional archaeologist, and I never looked back.

While I was in high school, I was able to find work each summer on archaeological digs in the Panhandle. After graduating from high school, I went to West Texas State University and got a bachelor's degree studying under Jack Hughes, who was widely recognized as the scholarly expert in Panhandle archaeology. I went on to Texas A&M University where I received my master's degree in anthropology in 1986. I then spent the next thirty-five years immersed in Texas archaeology.

So here is the bottom line: The Panhandle Plains is where I earned my first stripes in Texas archaeology. In my formative years, I was fortunate to have had many great opportunities to learn and do archaeology in the region that I love. Although my professional career took me in many different directions, I returned to work in the Panhandle every chance I got, and I cherish all my archaeological experiences there.

As you will see in the stories that follow, something always seems to be pulling me back toward my Panhandle archaeology roots.

Chapter 2

The M-Cross Ranch

Educator's Guide reference: Activity 3

J OHN: At an early age, I was fascinated by ranchers and cowboys because my mother told me stories about the ranchers and cowboys in her family. My kinfolks were among the first people to settle on the South Plains. They helped build the town of Estacado in 1880, and my great-grandfather was present the day Lubbock County was established.

After six years of college, I returned to the Panhandle. Between 1974 and 1981, I made my living as a cowboy, working on other people's ranches. By 1990, I had started a nice business writing and publishing Hank the Cowdog books. My wife Kris and I had saved up some money and started looking around for a little place in the country.

I happened to see an ad in *Livestock Weekly* for a ranch in the Canadian River Valley 40 miles south of Perryton. It was nine square miles of rough canyon country. In the heat of August, I spent two days riding horseback from one end of the ranch to the other accompanied by the realtor, Gene Scott of Amarillo. It happened that he had spent part of his childhood there, so he knew it well.

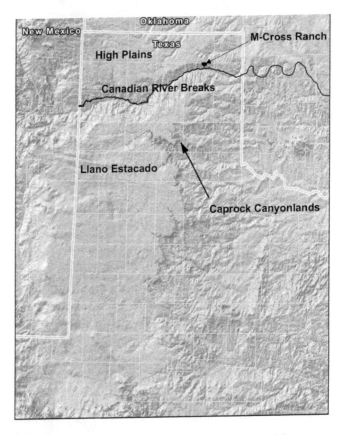

Figure 4: Topographic relief map of the Panhandle Plains. The concentration of resources—springs, plants, and wildlife—attracted prehistoric people to the Canadian River Breaks and Caprock Canyonlands. Map by Sandy Hannum.

The second day, we stopped on a hill overlooking a spring that seeped out of the base of the caprock. Gene pointed to a heavy scatter of quartzite rocks, pieces of bone, and flint chips—the debris of prehistoric people who had camped around the spring, probably for thousands of years.

He called it Indian Springs and told me that as a kid, he had hunted arrowheads on the slope above the spring. I wondered if he still had them. Probably not.

Once I had ridden the ranch and seen it all, I was hooked and became the owner of a spectacular piece of God's earth. Kris and I decided to call it the M-Cross Ranch, the brand my great-grandfather Joe Sherman had registered in Crosby County in 1887.

DOUG: There is one archaeological truth about the Texas Panhandle Plains region: the Llano Estacado could be a hostile environment at times, plagued by periodic droughts and occasional blizzards. That is why many prehistoric people chose to make their semi-permanent homes in the Canadian River Breaks or in the Caprock Canyonlands.

The archaeological sites found over most of the Llano Estacado are small ephemeral campsites where people stayed for short periods of time. If you want to find the big residential base camps or villages where people came back regularly and lived for months at a time, you have to go into the Canadian River Breaks or into the Caprock Canyonlands. Prehistoric people knew the river breaks and canyons had dependable freshwater springs, abundant wild plant foods, and plenty of game animals to hunt. John Erickson's M-Cross Ranch in Roberts County was this kind of place.

Chapter 3
Doug Wilkens

Educator's Guide reference: Activity 3

JOHN: After we bought the ranch, word spread that I had become the new owner and I began getting inquiries from artifact collectors who wanted permission to hunt on the property. I said no.

Something had changed in my thinking. I had become the guardian of ancient sites and wanted to protect them. I wanted to learn more about the long line of human beings who had occupied this rugged, beautiful piece of the earth before it passed into my hands.

One night I got a call from a fellow named Doug Wilkens. He had been about ten years behind me in school, rode broncs in high school rodeos, and played middle guard on the Perryton Rangers football team. After high school, he married Cara Sweigart from Balko and now worked for the oil company BP.

He was also a serious amateur archaeologist and a steward with the Texas Historical Commission (THC). He told me that the THC was planning to send a professional archaeologist up to the Panhandle to locate and record prehistoric sites in Roberts and Ochiltree Counties. A lot of archaeology had been done at Antelope Creek sites along the Canadian River about 50 miles west of my ranch and at the Buried City ruins 25 miles north of me, but the areas in between had remained a blank in the archaeological record. Nobody knew much about those hundreds of square miles, and Doug wondered if they could do a walking survey on my place. I said yes, of course. I went with them.

I knew of only one site—Indian Springs—so that was the first place we went. We found several others, but it's interesting that even under the guidance of a professional archaeologist, we didn't find the most intriguing site on the ranch: the prehistoric ghost town in West Pasture.

DOUG: For me, the 1988 Texas Archaeological Society's field school at the Buried City was one of those career-altering events because that was where I met Doug Wilkens. As you will read in this book, Wilkens plays a prominent role in the West Pasture archaeology story.

He had signed up for his first archaeological dig and was eager to learn. Digging together and sharing a passion for what we were finding and learning, the two Dougs forged a lasting friendship. I did not know it at the time, but that chance meeting would draw me back to Panhandle archaeology in ways I could never have predicted.

Chapter 4

Periods of Prehistoric Occupation

Educator's Guide reference: Activity 3

J OHN: For the first ten years we owned the ranch, I pursued an enlightened version of the arrowhead hunting I had done in Boy Scouts. I went to proven habitation sites such as Indian Springs and looked for artifacts, but instead of tossing them into the sock drawer, I kept them in specimen bags with the location written on them. I also separated them by function: points, tools, and pottery.

Strictly speaking, this wasn't archaeology—but it was moving in the right direction. Artifacts can give us hints about the age of the site and the group of people who occupied it. We have identified sites from three periods on the ranch: the Archaic period, the Woodland period, and the Plains Village period.

> **Archaic period** (2000 BC to AD 500): These nomadic hunter-gatherer people never stayed long in one place and built no permanent structures, so they didn't leave much behind. They used the *atlatl* instead of bows and

arrows, and they didn't make pottery. The main diagnostic of an Archaic site is the dart point, which is larger and not as finely made as the arrow points that came later, and of course an Archaic site contains no ceramic material.

Woodland period (AD 500 to 1100): Woodland people had acquired bow-and-arrow technology. The main diagnostic for a Woodland site is a triangular-shaped, corner-notched arrow point called a Scallorn point. Woodland sites contain a small amount of ceramic material, which means the Woodland people made pottery. Woodland houses are rare in my part of the Panhandle, but they've been reported in Late-Woodland sites to the south of us (Palo Duro Complex), in western Oklahoma (Custer Phase), and in southeastern Colorado (Graneros).

Plains Village period (AD 1100 or 1200 to 1450): Sites from this period tend to be rich in cultural material because people were living in permanent structures and producing trash. They hunted bison and raised corn, beans, and squash in garden plots. They lived in subterranean pit-houses and stored surplus crop foods in underground storage pits for use during the winter when food was scarce. The material culture includes two styles of side-notched points, the Washita and the Harrell, considerable pottery, four-bladed knives, bison-bone farming tools, and nonlocal materials such as shell beads and obsidian.

Indian Springs contains artifacts from all three periods, but it appears to be predominantly Woodland. The ghost town in West Pasture belongs to the Plains Village period.

DOUG: The rest of this book will focus on the Plains Village sites in the West Pasture and look at how they fit into the bigger picture of archaeology in the Texas Panhandle and in the Southern Plains.

The Plains Village period represents, for me at least, the most exciting period that an archaeologist can study in the Panhandle. This was a time when bison were plentiful, and people used bows and arrows to hunt them. People had perfected the art of making pottery. They built substantial houses and lived in villages as they planted and harvested crops.

People who preceded the Plains Villagers in the Panhandle were simple hunter-gatherers. They may have known something about crops, but they didn't get into farming in any meaningful way. They left behind sparse remains. Compared to these earlier sites, the Plains Village sites are rich in material culture. These sites are a giant playground for someone who loves Panhandle archaeology.

Chapter 5
Plains Village People

Educator's Guide reference: Activity 4

JOHN: Archaeologists have identified several Plains Village groups that occupied the South-Central Plains between AD 1200 and AD 1450.

Apishipa in eastern Colorado and northeast New Mexico

Upper Republican in Kansas and Nebraska

Antelope Creek in the Texas and Oklahoma Panhandles

Buried City in the northeastern Texas Panhandle

Odessa, Zimms, and Turkey Creek in western Oklahoma

Habitation materials from our sites show similarities to all these groups but also differences. We know they were pre-tribal, not the Kiowas or Comanches who occupied this region during the historic period. I learned about them by reading books and articles by Doug Boyd and other archaeologists.

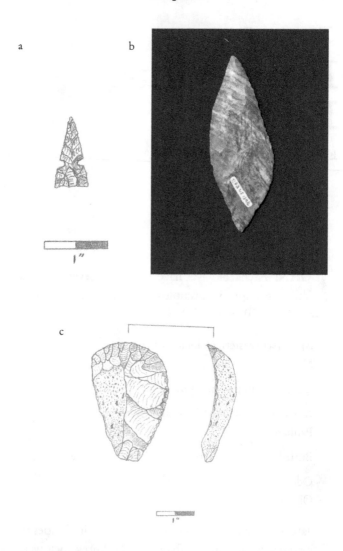

Figure 5a, b, c: The trio of bison hunting tools: (a) Washita arrow point for killing bison, (b) beveled knife for skinning bison, and (c) end scraper (hafted) used for processing hides. Drawings and photographs by Doug Wilkens.

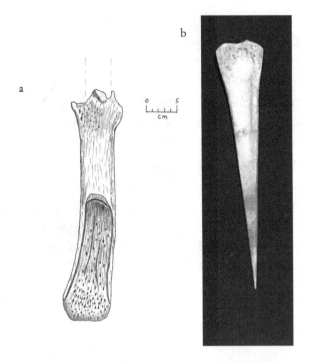

Figure 6a, b: Examples of bone tools found in Plains Village sites. (a) Modified buffalo tibia that was hafted onto a long wooden stick and used as a digging tool. (b) Bone awl (used like a leather punch) made from a deer leg bone. Drawing by Doug Boyd. Photograph by Doug Wilkens.

DOUG: Archaeologists use the term *Southern Plains Villagers* to refer to groups of people who lived a similar life-style. The list below specifies key traits that identify these Southern Plains Village cultures:

The people were semisedentary, meaning they lived in one village for much of the year and then roamed around hunting at other times.

They spent part of their time farming and part of their

time hunting buffalo with bows and arrows.

They organized their activities according to the seasons. They planted corn, beans, and squash in the spring and harvested them in the fall.

They were foragers, too. They hunted small animals, such as rabbits and birds, and they gathered and ate a variety of different native plants.

They made all their tools out of wood, flint rocks (chipped into shapes) and other stones, and bone.

They made pottery that has an unusual surface decoration called cordmarking. They made big round jars that archaeologists sometimes call bean pots. Wanna guess what they cooked in these jars?

Chapter 6
Curiosity

Educator's Guide reference: Activity 4

J OHN: From the very beginning, my interest in archaeology was driven by curiosity. Curiosity is something that no scientist will ever see under a microscope, but it's one of the traits that defines us as human beings and sets us apart from rocks and shrubs.

The simple definition of curiosity is *a love of knowledge* . . . not knowledge to make good grades or a pile of money, but knowledge for its own sake, for the thrill of learning. It's an invisible mysterious force that, through the ages, has caused our species to gaze into the sky and down at the dirt; to wonder why the grass grows and the birds sing, where we came from and why we're here. It has been the fuel behind worship, exploration, scientific discoveries, music, poetry, and great inventions.

I view it as a gift from our Creator who built ants and elephants, microbes and galaxies, and who understood that people need dogs.

I've always had my share of curiosity, and archaeology kicked it up to a higher level. I wanted to know more about the people who lived in my canyons and valleys before I arrived. What did they eat? Where did they live? What did they think about in the middle of the night? And how did they survive in a region where the weather can be hostile to human endeavors?

Doug Wilkens became the perfect companion in my dance with archaeology because he had the same tunes in his head and was driven by the same desire to push the boundaries of his knowledge.

Doug was an amateur like me, but he had participated in a number of controlled excavations and understood the importance of disciplined research. He was what we would call an avocational archaeologist: someone who is trained but not a professional. His service as a steward in the Texas Historical Commission and involvement in other organizations gave him access to professionals, their methods, and the body of written literature they had produced.

We have worked together in harmony for 30 years, and from the start we've had a division of labor. As the landowner and the guy who lives on the place, it's my job to look for things that 1) don't fit, 2) seem odd or out of context, and 3) suggest human activity.

When I find something, I pass it along to Wilkens. In the beginning, this meant that I called him on the phone and we discussed it. After we acquired smartphones, I was able to send him photographs and text messages, and we have made good use of emails. When he thinks I've found something of interest, he comes to the ranch and gives it a closer inspection.

Chapter 7

Burned Bone Fragments

Educator's Guide reference: Activity 4

JOHN: In the first years after we bought the ranch, I leased out the grazing rights to Perryton rancher Henry Hale. One morning I rode with him while he was feeding cattle in the East Pasture. As we drove across a stretch of flat prairie above the caprock, he pointed to several caliche rocks and said, "Those rocks shouldn't be there."

Henry didn't know anything about archaeology, but he was a careful observer of everything in his world, and he was right. Those rocks were out of context. They shouldn't have been there. I got out of the pickup and took a closer look. I found a number of fragments of burned bone on the surface. Burned bone is pretty solid proof of human activity, so I called Wilkens.

Notice that I didn't grab a shovel and start digging. I called someone who knew how to evaluate and preserve an archaeological site.

Wilkens came the next Saturday and concluded that the combination of rocks out of context and burned bone suggested that it might have been a house, although we agreed that on the flats and far from the nearest source of water and wood wasn't a place where a house should be.

Wilkens passed his report along to Billy Harrison and Rolla Shaller at the Panhandle-Plains Historical Museum, and in September we conducted a three-day excavation. What we found was not a house but a burial cyst that contained hundreds of fingernail-sized fragments of burned bone and one tooth that proved to be human.

We had stumbled upon what is known as a *secondary cremation burial*, which means that the body had been cremated at another location and the remains brought to this spot for burial. As far as I know, it's the only such burial ever reported in the Panhandle—and the site was discovered by a rancher who didn't know beans about archaeology.

Henry wasn't bothered that prehistoric people shouldn't have been there on the bald prairie, far from wood and water. That attitude introduced me to a crucial insight: when you think you know what you're seeing, you often miss what is actually there.

Regardless of whether you're an amateur or a professional, you must open your mind to *what is there*.

DOUG: Wilkens named this find the Caprock Cremation Burial. Even though it was fully investigated, it remains one of the biggest mysteries on the M-Cross Ranch. The fragmentary burned bones were examined by osteologists (bone scientists), and they determined the burned bones were of a young woman who was between 20 and 34 years old when she died.

We made two attempts to date the bones using the radiocarbon method, but both attempts failed because the burning had destroyed the carbon materials inside the bone that could be dated. While we suspect the woman lived during Plains Village times, we don't know for sure. If she was a Plains Villager, why was she singled out for cremation when most people were buried in graves in and around the village?

Archaeologists don't always find the answers we seek. But we keep on searching and learning.

Chapter 8
The Dykema Canyon Burial Site

Educator's Guide reference: Activity 4

JOHN: Another interesting discovery came about three years later. I was driving a D3 Caterpillar dozer in the East Pasture, trying to build a road in rugged Dykema Canyon. I wasn't scouting for sites, but I noticed several cracked quartzite rocks in a cattle trail. Quartzite rocks are a good indicator of habitation because prehistoric people used them for cooking by adding heated rocks to a bladder filled with water.

This didn't seem a likely spot for any kind of habitation (too rough), but I stopped the dozer and walked around. I noticed a white spot showing in the dirt and scraped on it with my pocketknife. I could see that it was bone and kept scraping. It got bigger and I figured it was a buffalo skull . . . until I exposed an eye socket that was definitely human.

I called Wilkens and gave him my report. It appeared that we had a burial in an area that was badly eroded and in danger of washing away. He came to the ranch the following Saturday, and we spent five hours removing the upper two-thirds of a human skeleton: a male of 35 years of age who lived around AD 660 in the Woodland period.

We found eight Scallorn-like arrow points in his chest area, so obviously he had been murdered. Through some miracle, the skull hadn't been crushed by the hooves of cattle and remained in perfect condition, including a full set of teeth.

Again, notice that I didn't do the excavation myself. I knew I wasn't qualified.

DOUG: The Dykema burial is a great example that illustrates the importance of context in archaeology. Think of context as a group of artifacts found together, and the relationships between the items have meaning.

What if archaeologists dug up the kitchen area in your house one thousand years from now? If all we found was a single fork, it wouldn't reveal much. But if we found clusters of food jars and cans, pots and pans, forks and knives, and plates and bowls all in one area, it would tell us that area was used for storing, preparing, and consuming food. We could learn what your family was eating and make educated guesses as to how you were cooking meals.

We learned so much from the Dykema burial because it was excavated properly to document the precise positions of the human bones and the arrow points, and how these things related to the burial pit.

Once the artifacts were removed from the ground, archaeologists studied the arrow points under a microscope, and osteologists cleaned and examined the skeletal remains. They found tiny slice marks on a clavicle (collarbone) created when an arrow entered the man's chest, and they found a tiny fragment of flint—the tip of one of the

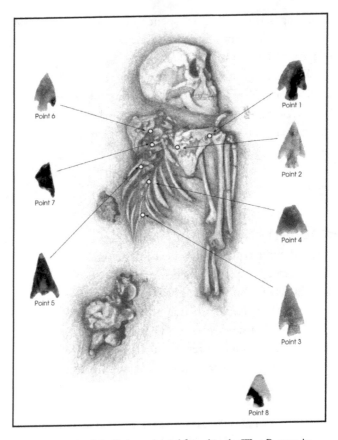

Figure 7: Sketch of the Dykema burial found in the West Pasture in 1998. The lower half of the body had eroded away, but the upper half contained abundant evidence that this man was killed. Image compiled by Sandy Hannum using drawing by Ryan Wilkens and arrow point photographs by Doug Wilkens.

arrow points—that had broken off in a vertebra (one of the spine bones of his lower back).

We dated the bones and examined the chemistry of the teeth to learn about this man's diet. Guess what? He had a general hunter-gatherer diet and didn't eat any corn. This diet is characteristic of the Plains Woodland period.

To really understand context, think about this for a moment. What if Erickson hadn't seen something odd and stopped the bulldozer to take a closer look? What could we have learned if the burial had been dozed out of the ground before it was discovered?

If all meaningful context information had been lost, we wouldn't have been able to reconstruct the story of how the man in the Dykema burial lived and died some 1,300 years ago.

It is also important to note that in excavating this human burial, we followed all the state laws pertaining to cemeteries and unmarked graves, and the Dykema burial remains will be reburied in a safe place on the ranch.

Chapter 9
Douglas K. Boyd

J OHN: One day in the summer of 2000, I was riding horseback in a sand draw in West Pasture. To my right, I noticed a cut bank about twelve feet high, a flat surface that centuries of floodwater had carved out of a sandhill.

In the past, I had found bison bones in such settings, so I stopped and gave it a closer inspection. I was surprised to see a chunk of burned wood maybe 12 inches long, showing beneath seven feet of sand. That struck me as odd. Charcoal fragments are usually evidence of human occupation, but what was it doing under a pile of sand?

It wasn't my job to understand, only to report, so I called Wilkens. He said, "Hmmm." It happened that an archaeologist friend, Doug Boyd, planned to be in the Panhandle a few weeks later and Wilkens brought him out to look at the site. Boyd paced back and forth in front of the cut bank, pulling his chin and studying the profile. After a few minutes, he whirled around.

"Boys, we're looking at a prehistoric house that's been cut in half." Like a professor at a blackboard, he used his trowel to mark a faint line of dark soil that formed a basin shape. "That's the house." He pointed to an urn-shaped impression in the center. "That's a clay-lined hearth." He pointed to the chunk of charcoal. "That's a piece of burned roof timber. This is a burned pit-house."

I was surprised. I could have stared at that profile for a week and never seen a house. That was a lesson on the importance of soil changes: an amateur sees only dirt; a trained archaeologist sees the subtle changes in soil that say, "Something different is happening here." Boyd had excavated several pit-houses at Palo Duro Complex sites around Post, Turkey, and Clarendon, and he saw it immediately. Boyd and Wilkens decided to name our new discovery "Hank's House" in honor of the literary character who was making my ranch payments, and they began planning an excavation.

DOUG: It made perfect sense to me to suggest we name a buried prehistoric house on John Erickson's ranch after the main character in the Hank the Cowdog books. We kicked the idea around during our evening porch talk, and it stuck.

We assigned character names to other prehistoric houses we investigated, and later on you'll hear about Drover's and Pete's Houses. We will continue this practice as we dig at more places on the ranch. Fortunately, we won't run out of character names because old Hank has made a lot of friends, acquaintances, and adversaries in his many adventures.

Just to set the record straight, I spoke up first to declare it a burned pit-house, but Wilkens gets equal credit for discovering it. We both worked in silence for a while as we troweled the creek cut bank smooth. We glanced back and forth, smiling at each other because we both knew what it was, without having to say a word.

That was one of those wonderful "aha" moments (in Panhandle-speak it's "aw haw") in archaeology that I will never forget.

Chapter 9

The three of us will always remember July 16, 2000, as the day we discovered Hank's House. That was the day when we realized the significance of this find and started planning for a formal archaeological dig.

That was my introduction to the West Pasture on the M-Cross Ranch. I didn't know it at the time, but it was also the beginning of an archaeological adventure that would unfold there over two decades.

Chapter 10

What Archaeology Is All About

J OHN: Boyd served as the Principal Investigator (PI) for the Hank's House dig and supervised a crew of six to ten volunteers. We conducted several week-long digs in November, December, and January, and excavated the house down to sterile soil, which is the dirt below the level of habitation.

Hank's House gave me my first taste of field archaeology, so this might be a good place to talk about what archaeologists hope to accomplish in their work, using Boyd as an example. I've worked with him for twenty years on M-Cross Ranch projects and have developed a great respect for his expertise in the four areas that define the profession: scholarship, excavation, analysis, and writing.

> **Scholarship**. We often think of archaeologists as people who pull artifacts out of the dirt and put them on display in a museum, but before they scrape a trowel across the dirt, they need to understand the context of each particular site and how it fits into the archaeological record of the region.

That knowledge comes from scholarship: studying articles and books that describe the work that has been done in the past. Boyd has mastered the literature. He seems to have read everything that has been written about archaeology on the Southern Plains and could talk with authority about prehistoric cultures in New Mexico, Arizona, the Mississippi River Valley, and the Northern Plains as well.

> **Excavation** involves moving dirt around with a shovel and trowel, shaking it through a screen, and recovering cultural material: tools, pottery, bone, shells, fragments of burned daub, and even something as small as charred kernels of corn. It's hard physical work in summer heat and winter cold, and it's nothing a slacker would want to try. Boyd is jackrabbit-tough and excels at it. He seems immune to fatigue and unpleasant weather.

Excavation also involves scientific precision: laying out grids, recording levels, keeping careful records, photographing wall profiles, and collecting artifacts and soil samples. It would be hard to overstate the importance of this process, because once an excavation is completed, very little remains except a hole. Moving dirt around is pointless if you don't keep careful records of what you've done, and Boyd is a scrupulous recorder of details.

> **Analysis**. The excavation of Hank's House produced several types of material that Boyd sent to experts who did detailed analysis. Charcoal samples showed that the posts and framework were made of local juniper trees. Samples of bone showed a diet of bison, deer, rabbits, and birds. Shell fragments told that the occupants were eating freshwater mussels. Dirt from the floor and ash from the hearth revealed a diet that included

wild plums, cactus, the seeds of wild plants, and locally raised corn. The charred corn gave us a reliable Carbon 14 date of approximately AD 1300.

Writing. Some archaeologists excel at excavation, scholarship, or analysis but aren't so good at writing and publishing their results. In fact, it's not uncommon for projects, even big ones, to go unreported for decades, and some will never find their way into printed form. Hence, a huge expenditure of time and labor goes into excavations that yield hardly a drop of information. That's too bad, because information is the most important artifact in any excavation: a written record of the data collected at the site plus an interpretation of what it means.

Doug Boyd is a very good writer. His work is well documented and written in prose that is clear and precise, uncluttered by the kind of obscurity that sometimes creeps into academic writing. I've always been impressed by his ability to translate science into readable English.

Anyone who wants to learn about the archaeology of the Panhandle-Plains region should start with Boyd's *Caprock Canyonlands Archaeology: A Synthesis of the Late Prehistoric and History of Lake Alan Henry and the Texas Panhandle-Plains, Volume II*. It was the first book I read on the subject, and I've read it several times since. The bad news is that Boyd's work, like most writing on archaeology, is hard to find. That's a shame. I've often thought that his *Synthesis* should be in every library in Texas.

DOUG: In my business, the archaeological reports produced by publicly funded Cultural Resource Management (CRM) projects are often called "gray" literature. This name is fitting because, for most reports, few hard copies are printed and distributed, and they are hard to find. Things have been changing for the better in recent years as entire libraries have gone digital and are available online.

CRM archaeology reports have become more widely available and are relatively easy for other professional and academic archaeologists to find. Many of them are now available to the general public on a website that doesn't require a password. It's called the Index of Texas Archaeology: Open Access Gray Literature of the Lone Star State.

There it is. I have let the cat out of the bag. Now everyone can have access to most of the CRM gray literature reports in Texas. It is true that some of them can only be described as dull, but there are some really amazing reports there too.

One other great public resource is a website called Texas Beyond History, which is a public education service of the Texas Archaeological Research Laboratory at the University of Texas at Austin. It is a great place to start learning about important archaeological sites all over Texas. It's well illustrated with lots of maps and photos of sites, features, and artifacts.

There is even a special exhibit with lots of information about the Plains Villagers and one of the West Pasture sites you will read about in this book. If you want to know more about Texas archaeology when you're done reading this book, you can go check it out at www.texasbeyondhistory.net.

Chapter 11
Hank's House

Educator's Guide reference: Activity 5

JOHN: Now let's get back to that unusual cut bank feature in West Pasture. Boyd and Wilkens put out the word in the Panhandle archaeology community that we would be digging a new site. They gathered up a crew that included experienced amateurs, a few rookies like me and Kris, and some professionals, including Brett Cruse from Austin and Reggie Wiseman from New Mexico.

Our first task was to remove seven feet of sand that covered the house, and we did it with a device that makes archaeologists uneasy: a bulldozer.

Archaeologists work primarily with dental tools and brushes. They measure levels of dirt in centimeters, so they cringe when a dozer shows up. A dozer eats centimeters of dirt for a snack, but if you need to move cubic yards of sand, it's the right tool for the job. The alternative is human labor, and there are better uses for volunteer labor than grunting out tons of sterile overburden—that is, upper fill that doesn't contain artifacts—with shovels and buckets.

When I began pushing sand at Hank's site, Boyd was right there to supervise every swipe of the blade. He checked the floor of the trench for changes in soil color and texture, and when he saw the first signs of charcoal flecking and smears, he gave me the sign to back the dozer out of the trench. At that point, we switched to shovels and trowels and continued removing the last few inches of the sandy overburden.

Boyd knew, judging by the amount of ash, darkened soil, and charcoal in the upper layers, that this was going to be a burned house. In the bitter cold of December and January, we exposed the remaining one-half of a pit-house, which included the floor, a central depressed channel, half of a clay-lined central hearth, two of the four original central support posts, an east-facing entryway, and an outline of charred posts around the perimeter.

DOUG: Doing good archaeology depends on using the right tool for the job. There are times when you need to move a lot of dirt quickly, and a big digging machine is the only way to go. I've used backhoes, trackhoes, Gradalls, bulldozers, and maintainers to dig windows into the ground and search for buried remains.

Once the big machines have done their job and have removed the overburden, archaeologists must slow down their digging and use smaller tools to expose artifacts and features in place. In our excavation at Hank's House, we carefully exposed and mapped the features that defined the house. We also found small artifacts in place on the house floor. Using bamboo digging sticks and soda straws to blow away the dirt in one area near the south wall, we carefully exposed fragile tubes of charred grass that were later identified as yellow Indiangrass (botanists call it by its genus and species name *Sorghastrum nutans*).

Because it was found directly on the house floor, we think the grass may have been used as a sleeping mat.

Chapter 12
Burned Houses

J OHN: To a novice like me, it wasn't obvious that a burned house can be a bonanza for archaeologists, so let's talk about that. First, we have to consider that a house like Hank's was built of 100 percent organic material: dirt, mud, grass, and a framework of cedar and juniper.

Over the course of 700 years, an unburned house decomposes and leaves nothing behind but soil and maybe fragments of the central hearth. Hence, an unburned pit-house is almost invisible to excavators. Unless they're looking for a slight darkening of the soil, they might miss it entirely.

Our burned house, on the other hand, left a wealth of evidence because—I had never thought of this—organic material that has been exposed to fire doesn't decompose. Charcoal remains charcoal for thousands of years. In Hank's House, we were able to recover charred seeds and bones that gave us information about diet. We also recovered charred wood, charred posts, and hardened daub and plaster that yielded excellent information about the architecture of the house.

Our sharp-eyed PI noticed something else that only an expert would have caught: a thick layer of heat-altered soil *on top* of charred wood, an unusual feature indicating that this was an earth-covered structure. That was an important observation, and we will have more to say about it later on.

When you find a house that burned seven centuries ago, you naturally wonder what caused the fire. Boyd had to find the answer in the excavated material. Here were the scenarios he considered:

Accidental burning. This could be the result of a cooking fire inside the house or a prairie fire on the outside. The evidence would show that the residents fled the house, leaving tools, pots, and food in place on the floor.

Warfare. Here, you look for evidence of violence: weapons, human remains, and signs of conflict and flight.

Intentional burning. After occupying a house for fifteen or twenty years, residents considered it unsafe or maybe it was infested with vermin. The evidence for this would be: they cleaned it out, everybody left, and they burned it.

DOUG: We had to consider all the possibilities for why Hank's House burned, and a violent attack was one of them. I could tell you a pretty grisly story about a pit-house that was burned with people inside it and the ten human "trophy skulls" that were placed into a pit inside that house. This was a real event that happened in the Texas Panhandle at about the same time that Hank's House was occupied, but I won't go into that story now.

Let's just say that there is a fair amount of archaeological evidence for violence in the Southern Plains during the Plains Village period.

While it might be tempting to jump to a conclusion that Hank's House was burned during a violent attack,

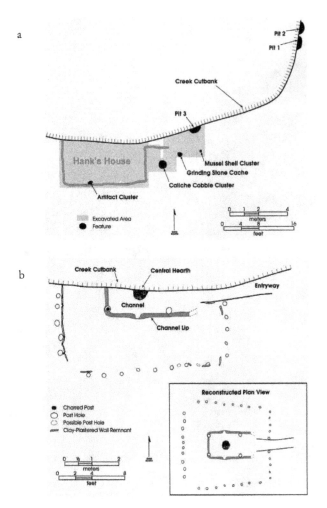

Figure 8a, b: Plan drawing of Hank's House excavation. Map by Sandy Hannum.

archaeologists have to be objective and follow the evidence wherever it leads us. If the house was burned by a raiding war party or if it burned down accidentally, there would have been lots of artifacts scattered on the floor.

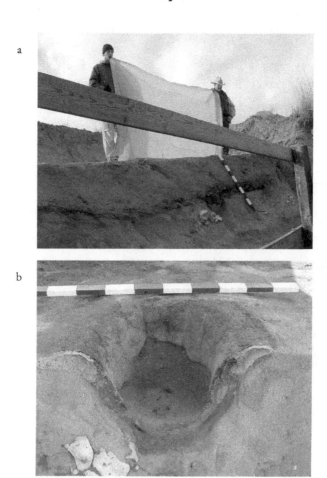

Figure 9a, b: Photographs of Hank's House floor. (a) Central hearth and burned debris before excavation, with Mark Erickson (left) and John Erickson (right) holding a tarp to provide shade for close-up photos. (b) Central hearth after it was completely excavated. The top of the hearth was plastered with clay. Photographs by Doug Boyd.

There would have been lots of pottery sherds from cooking vessels that got broken.

There weren't. All the evidence in Hank's House pointed in a different direction—an orderly abandonment. We also had one more piece of evidence that was pretty crucial. We had found a circular notch dug into the floor plaster where an extra support post had been added to prop up the roof. This told us that Hank's House had been occupied long enough for the roof to begin to sag.

Our best guess is that people lived in Hank's House for eight to twelve years before it was abandoned and burned. At some point in the lifespan of this house, it became too dilapidated to repair. It was easier to burn it down and start over by building a new house.

Chapter 13
Why All the Sand?

J OHN: Before ending our discussion of Hank's House, we need to address one last question: why was it buried under seven feet of sand?

The best speculation of Boyd, Wilkens, and others was that after the house was abandoned, the Texas Panhandle experienced at least one—maybe several—periods of catastrophic drought. Strong winds scoured the dry beds of tributary streams and possibly the Canadian River, depositing the sand on nearby prairie. Believe it or not, that erosional event involving thousands of tons of soil could have occurred in one or two days. I can remember dust storms in 1955 when sand dunes buried barbed wire fences in one frightful day. Such is the awesome power of wind.

Dr. Charles Frederick, a geoarchaeologist who joined our team in 2006, studied the profiles of several backhoe trenches in West Pasture. He found fertile soil buried beneath hills of sand. In the 1300s, those might have been the fields where our West Pasture folks were raising their corn.

Figure 10: Geoarchaeologist Charles Frederick standing next to a back-hoe trench that revealed a sequence of sand dune deposits on top of the alluvial terrace along a creek. By studying the layers of deposits and soil formation evidence, Frederick was able to reconstruct the "life history" of the West Pasture stream valley. Photograph by Doug Boyd.

DOUG: When Charles began working on the West Pasture project, he wanted to understand the landscape of the whole stream valley (the big-picture stuff) and the deposits at each of the sites where we were digging (the small-picture stuff).

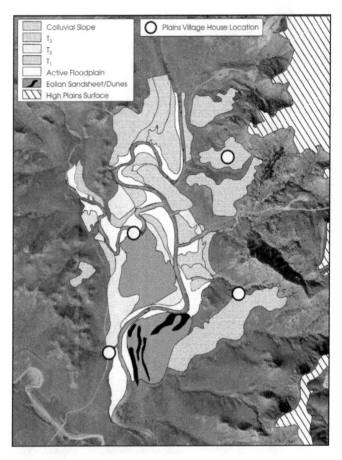

Figure 11: Map of West Pasture valley showing the ages of different landforms. Each pattern is different and represents a unique landform, such as an alluvial (river) terrace or eolian (windblown) sand dunes, deposited during specific time periods. This type of map helps archaeologists predict where different kinds of archaeological remains may be found. Map by Charles Frederick.

He wanted to know how and when all the big landscape features were formed, which in turn helps us understand why we find buried archaeological remains in the places we do.

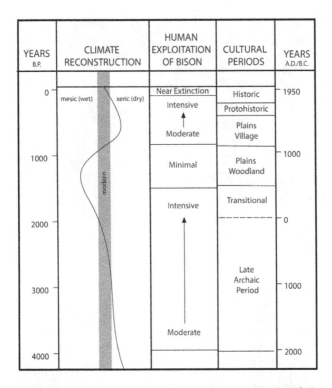

Figure 12: Chronological graph comparing climate change (rainfall), bison populations, and cultural periods over the last 4,000 years. The Texas Panhandle climate has fluctuated over time, causing corresponding changes in prairie grasslands, which in turn caused fluctuations in the bison population. Graph by Sandy Hannum.

Charles put in a lot of miles walking across West Pasture and looking at everything from the caprock rim to the bottom of the creek bed. He looked at every creek cut bank and road cut he could find, and he dug backhoe trenches to look at buried deposits he couldn't see.

He collected soil samples from each deposit and then studied those samples in his laboratory to determine how each deposit formed. Sediment deposited by the wind looks

Figure 13: Photograph of sand dunes encroaching on a farmhouse in the Texas Panhandle during the Great Depression. Named "Dust Bowl Farm," this photo was taken by Dorothea Lange in June 1938 at a farm near Dalhart. Photograph is from the US Library of Congress, Farm Security Administration Collection (https://www.loc.gov/item/2017770620/).

very different from sediment laid down by a creek during a flood. Charles also used a variety of dating techniques to determine the ages of the various deposits and landforms.

Slowly, over the course of several years and after examining and dating dozens of samples, Charles began to see patterns in the data. He began to see how the climate in Roberts County had changed over the last 3,000 years and to understand when the West Pasture stream terraces and sand dunes were formed. The dating of when sand dunes formed was particularly important because it identified long periods of extremely dry conditions, perhaps like the dust bowl days during the Great Depression.

Why All the Sand?

Geomorphology (the study of soil and stratigraphy) can be a pretty complicated thing to wrap your brain around, but Charles makes it look easy.

Chapter 14
Beyond Hank's House

J OHN: When we concluded the excavation of Hank's House in January 2001, Boyd and Wilkens left the site with bags of soil and artifacts, boxes of burned wood and daub, and hundreds of pages of records. Over the next several years, they cataloged the material, submitted samples for analysis, and wrote up their field notes. In time, both published good articles that appeared in professional journals.

The last day at the site, as we were walking through tall sagebrush on our way to the pickup, Boyd stopped and pointed toward the prairie country to the east. He said, "You know what? We could have houses all over that area."

I must admit that sounded odd to me. In the ten years I had owned the ranch, it had never occurred to me that I should look for artifacts in that area. Every amateur arrowhead hunter knows that prehistoric people camped and lived close to a reliable source of drinking water, and the south half of West Pasture had *none*: no springs, no water, and no cottonwood trees, which meant no people, no arrowheads, and no houses. That line of reasoning will be correct 99 percent of the time.

What lay behind Boyd's statement was his realization that the prairie we were seeing in 2001 was not the same as the one that existed in 1300. We had just excavated a house that had no obvious water source, but if people occupied Hank's House, they had springs close by. And there might have been other springs and other houses not so far away.

Boyd's statement turned out to be prophetic, and it completely changed the course of our investigations.

While Boyd and Wilkens labored over the material we had recovered from Hank's House, I had my own projects to pursue. The information we had unearthed in the excavation sparked my interest and spurred me into reading articles and books on Panhandle archaeology. For me, that was a big step. I've always been a slow reader and one without much patience for technical writing. Once again, curiosity had to drag the donkey down the trail.

Boyd and Wilkens began sending me books and articles, and I plowed through them. It was difficult at first but got easier with practice. I read Boyd's book on archaeology of the Panhandle and South Plains, then books and articles by Brett Cruse, Chris Lintz, Richard Drass, Robert Brooks, Scott Brosowske, David Hughes, Jack Hughes, Robert Campbell, Peggy Flynn, and others.

I underlined passages that seemed to relate to our research, wrote notes in the margins, and typed up summaries. Each source added to my understanding of the people who occupied the Southern Plains during the Plains Village period.

All the primary sources agreed that several similar but distinct groups of sedentary farmers occupied the South-Central Plains between AD 1200 and 1450. We've already seen the list, but let's take another look at it:

Apishipa in eastern Colorado and northeast New Mexico

Upper Republican in Kansas and Nebraska

Antelope Creek in the Texas and Oklahoma Panhandles

Buried City in the northeast Texas Panhandle

Odessa, Zimms, and Turkey Creek in western Oklahoma

Most archaeology maps showed the entire Texas Panhandle and part of the Oklahoma Panhandle in the Antelope Creek occupation zone. One of the primary diagnostic traits of Antelope Creek was that they built houses with foundations and walls made of rock, known as stone enclosures.

The first Anglo settlers in the region spotted those circles, rectangles, and ovals of stone right away, and those were also the earliest sites excavated by archaeologists, first at the Buried City ruins south of Perryton and later at the heavily occupied zone around the Alibates flint quarries north of Amarillo.

From the start, our team assumed that my ranch lay in the Antelope Creek occupation zone (as it was defined at that time), and that any structures we found would be stone enclosures. Hence, we thought our research would add to the large body of literature that had already been compiled on Antelope Creek.

But wait. Our first house wasn't a stone enclosure, but a pit-house with picket-post construction.

Hmm. We didn't fit the model. We weren't aware of it at the time, but *not* fitting the models of Panhandle archaeology would become a common theme in our research. That's why Boyd invented his own semi-scientific term for

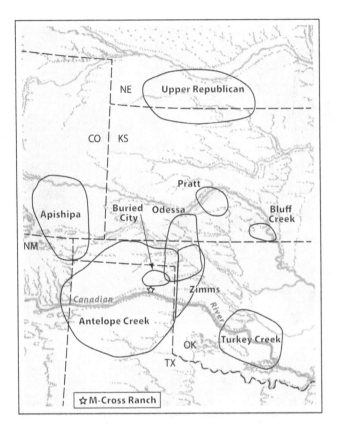

Figure 14a: Regional map showing the location of the West Pasture and the archeologically defined Plains Village–period culture areas surrounding it. Map by Sandy Hannum.

our discoveries: "Typical West Pasture." That was a humorous way of saying, "This doesn't fit the models!"

DOUG: All scientists work with theories, models, and hypotheses. Archaeologists are no exception, and we create models of how we think prehistoric people lived in different areas, based on the evidence we find.

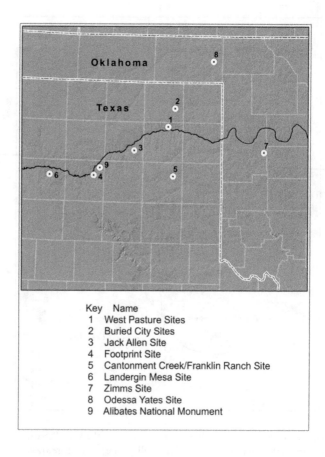

Key   Name
1   West Pasture Sites
2   Buried City Sites
3   Jack Allen Site
4   Footprint Site
5   Cantonment Creek/Franklin Ranch Site
6   Landergin Mesa Site
7   Zimms Site
8   Odessa Yates Site
9   Alibates National Monument

Figure 14b: Regional map showing important Plains Village sites in the Texas Panhandle and western Oklahoma. Map by Sandy Hannum.

When we find lots of evidence that doesn't fit one of our models, it's time to go back to our model-building drawing board. That's what happened right away in the West Pasture.

I had been taught that the Antelope Creek people (the old term for the Plains Villagers in the Panhandle) used big rock slabs to create wall foundations when they built their pit-houses. The first house I saw in the West Pasture didn't have foundation rocks. Why not? We needed to know the answer.

Chapter 15
Picket–Post Houses in Oklahoma and Texas

Educator's Guide reference: Activity 6

J OHN: We scoured the literature and compiled a list of picket-post structures within 200 miles of our location. Our search revealed that picket-post houses were common to the north of us in Kansas and Nebraska (Upper Republican sites) and in Paoli, Turkey Creek, and Zimms sites in western Oklahoma.

We found a few obscure references to picket-post houses in the Antelope Creek occupation zone: Jack Allen, Footprint III, Courson A, and Cantonment Creek. In the literature, scholars regarded them as variants on the standard Antelope Creek or Buried City stone-enclosed house and little more was said about them. Apparently, Panhandle archaeologists didn't know a great deal about picket-post houses, which could mean a) there weren't many in our region or b) they were harder to find than stone enclosures and had gone unnoticed.

We didn't know which might be true, but we were dead sure that we had found one in the West Pasture.

The layout and design of Hank's House bore a strong resemblance to houses in western Oklahoma. We began to wonder if our picket-post structure might point to a migration of people or ideas from the east rather than from Antelope Creek hamlets to the west. This raised questions about the prevailing model of a monolithic Antelope Creek influence over the entire Panhandle.

Jack Hughes had wondered the same thing. In his field notes, he commented on the similarities between pottery samples in eastern Panhandle sites to those found in Upper Republican sites in Kansas and Nebraska.

We lacked the evidence to prove a direct link to other cultural groups and it wasn't our job to attempt it, but we were certainly beginning to wonder how closely our West Pasture people were tied to the core area of Antelope Creek occupation around Lake Meredith . . . if at all.

DOUG: All this talk about prehistoric pit-house architecture may seem kind of odd at first. Why should we care about the seemingly minor difference in how the walls and roofs of prehistoric pit-houses were built?

Modern architects use a blueprint to show the plan of each house they build. Your cultural beliefs, passed down to you from your parents, dictate the materials you would use to build your house and most or all of the architectural details—the shape and arrangement of the walls, floor, doorways, and roof. People even arrange the interior of their houses according to their cultural beliefs.

Prehistoric people had a mental blueprint that they followed. The kind of houses that they built have been a very public display of their culture. If you want to understand any group of people living around the world, look at the houses they live in and the clothes they wear. More than anything else, houses and clothing are visible displays of peoples' identities. Under normal circumstances, prehistoric clothing seldom gets preserved in archaeological sites. Prehistoric houses rarely do either, but when pit-house walls and roofs got burned, their architectural details could be beautifully preserved.

Chapter 16
Scouting for Sites

J OHN: After the excavation of Hank's House, I changed tactics. Instead of collecting artifacts, I began looking for the kind of stone-enclosed houses that, according to conventional thinking, should have been there. We knew that stone enclosures had been reported on ranches 5 to 25 miles from West Pasture and felt certain that we had them. As Chief Location Scout, I considered it my job to find them.

Whenever the opportunity arose, I took off walking across pastures, looking at the ground for signs of human occupation. I concentrated my efforts on West Pasture, the area that lay on both sides of West Fork of Pickett Ranch Creek, from Indian Springs on the north to my property line on the south.

This was the place I had never thought of scouting until Boyd had said, "We could have houses all over that area."

In the early going, I was looking for surface debris: reddish quartzite rocks, flint chips, charcoal, bone fragments, and sometimes small pieces of pottery. That cultural material transmitted the message that *somebody has been here*.

I paid close attention to small piles of fresh dirt that gophers had brought to the surface. Oftentimes, gopher mounds contain habitation debris or ashy soil that doesn't appear anywhere else on the surface.

Where I found a scatter of cultural debris, I began looking for rocks on the surface that were 1) out of context and weren't part of a natural formation; 2) were of a size that could have been carried in by a human; and 3) might be part of the foundation line of a stone-enclosed house.

I marked all out-of-context stones with a pin flag and sometimes probed the soil around them with a sharpened rod, looking for buried rocks that might form a foundation line. If Wilkens thought the rocks were cultural, he recorded the sites with GPS readings.

Today, those wanderings of a curious amateur have taken on the quality of a huge practical joke. I spent hours—months—hiking around the south half of West Pasture looking for Antelope Creek-type stone-enclosed houses . . . and found *none*, not one stone-enclosed house.

What I found instead was a trickle of evidence that led to our discovery of a prehistoric pit-house village that had been buried for hundreds of years and had left only a small amount of cultural material on the surface.

Those out-of-context stones I flagged *were* cultural. They identified the sites as habitation zones, but they weren't part of walls or foundation-lines of structures. Several rock clusters marked burial cairns. Others lay on the surface near buried pit-houses, and we really don't know why they were there or what purpose they served, but they pointed to some kind of human activity.

DOUG: Ranchers make the best archaeological scouts. All they need is a little interest in the past and to pay attention as they drive, walk, or ride horseback around their ranch.

When a crew of archaeologists does a typical survey to search for evidence of sites, we line up facing the same direction, spaced out about 15 to 25 feet apart, and everyone walks the same direction in these parallel rows. We walk back and forth, just like plowing a field. We usually walk over any given piece of land only one time, and we may dig a few shovel test holes and screen the dirt that comes out. We can, and do, miss things in our surveys.

Ranch owners and ranch workers, on the other hand, are on the land every day and at different times of the day. They pass over the same ranch roads and cattle trails regularly. They see what comes out of the ground when they dig fence postholes. They see the patches of bare ground right after wind and rainstorms have passed through.

In this way, observant ranchers are doing an archaeological survey every time they go outside.

Erickson began to look at his land differently anytime he was out doing ranch work or when he was scouting for sites. Over time, he trained his eyes to see things that looked out of place or not natural. That's precisely what an archaeologist does.

Erickson taught me that you can see a lot of archaeology from a four-wheeler. I'd never done that until I met him. It's also kinda fun. I want to try surveying on horseback someday too.

Chapter 17
Drover's House

J **OHN:** As our knowledge of West Pasture grew, we divided it into four zones: Indian Springs, Hank A and B, Whistling Squaw, and Three Toes. One afternoon, I was tramping around Whistling Squaw, half a mile east of Hank's House, scouting a swath of prairie that followed a gentle slope from the base of Hodges Mesa down to the dry bed of West Fork of Pickett Ranch Creek.

I found a small amount of cultural material on the surface—flint chips, bone fragments, and quartzite rock—but nothing significant.

Then, up near the highest point, I noticed a patch of darkened soil that didn't match the color of the soil around it. I bent down and scraped it with my pocketknife. It revealed ash and charcoal, a reliable indicator of human activity. I called Wilkens and he came to the ranch a few days later.

He scraped the dark soil with his trowel and looked up. "Erickson, that's burned daub. We've got another pit-house and it's sitting right here on the surface. I can't believe we could be so lucky."

I looked closer at the dark chunks he had exposed with his trowel. Sure enough, they bore a close resemblance to the hundreds of burned daub fragments we had found in

Hank's House. If we had been trying to guess where people might have built a house, this location would have been the least likely place. It was too high up the slope and too far from any source of water.

It fit Boyd's category of "Typical West Pasture."

Boyd decided to call it Drover's House after Hank the Cowdog's little pal in the books, and in 2004, he assembled a crew of volunteers who began the first of several excavations that stretched over a three-year period. Sure enough, it was another burned pit-house, an exact replica of Hank's House, only this one contained a wealth of research material about its design and structure. We will come back to that later.

DOUG: By 2004, Erickson had become a top-notch avocational archaeologist with a keen eye for anything that looked out of place or unnatural. A small patch of discolored soil was what led to his discovery of Drover's House.

When they took me to see the site, I was amazed because there was so little evidence on the surface. But Wilkens was right about the tiny pieces of fired daub. They were the smoking gun, and they were pointing us to another burned pit-house.

As a side note, you may be wondering about our tradition of naming the prehistoric houses investigated on the M-Cross Ranch after the characters in John Erickson's Hank the Cowdog books. This came about quite accidentally, but in hindsight it was inevitable. As soon as we began investigating the first house on the ranch, we dubbed it Hank's House, and the name stuck. For the next big investigation, we named the place Drover's House, followed by one we named Pete's House after Hank's nemesis, Pete the barn cat. It wouldn't be fair to name them all after dogs, right?

Chapter 17

When we dig more prehistoric houses on the ranch, we plan to name them after some of the other characters, like the coyotes Missy and Scraunch or the buzzards Wallace and Junior. There are plenty of characters to choose from in the Hank books, so we should be set for quite a few more years.

Chapter 18

Geophysical Research

J OHN: The discovery of Drover's House moved us a step closer to Doug Boyd's prediction that we might have more prehistoric houses at Whistling Squaw and Three Toes, and we had begun to suspect that they wouldn't be the kind of stone enclosures I had been looking for. They were likely to be replicas of Hank's and Drover's houses: buried pit-houses with very little cultural debris on the surface.

To help us find evidence of buried structures, Boyd brought in technical people who did a remote sensing survey with a magnetometer, a computerized instrument that was mounted on wheels like a lawnmower and could detect hidden features below the surface. They laid out grids with ropes and stakes and the operator pushed the device along the rope lines.

The device took readings of magnetic changes in the soil down to eighteen inches, and a computer recorded anomalies in the soil on a digital map. Burned soil showed up on the screen as a dark spot, and the device even picked up faint rectangular shapes that suggested unburned pit-houses.

Downslope from Drover's House, we tested two of the anomalies. One turned out to be a pit, loaded with fourteenth-century trash. Archaeologists love going through other peoples' trash, and this one yielded a great deal of good information.

Boyd predicted that the second anomaly would be the central hearth of an unburned pit-house, and he was right. Thanks to precise digital information, we were able to find and expose the hearth as well as a faint shadow of darker soil, all that remained of a house someone had lived in seven hundred years ago. Boyd named this one Pete, after another character in the Hank books.

Across the creek at Three Toes—a half-mile southwest of Drover—we did a core test of another anomaly the magnetometer had picked up. We found big chunks of charcoal, a sure sign that the probe had hit a burned post. Boyd opened several test units and exposed a wall that contained burned posts, burned daub, and wall plaster. It was another burned pit-house.

Meanwhile, Wilkens was working nearby testing another anomaly. This one turned out to be a pit that contained a cache of bison bones and two large basin-shaped metates that had been used for grinding corn. Each metate had a hole knocked in the basin's center, an indication it had been "killed," perhaps on the death of the woman who had used it in better times.

DOUG: I am a big fan of remote sensing. It doesn't always work, but the magnetometer has proven to be an amazing tool for finding buried features at our West Pasture sites. The magnetometer data led us right to a beautiful fire pit in the center of Pete's House, and we would not have found this house without it.

In typical West Pasture fashion, Pete wasn't going to give up his secrets easily, and he had some more lessons to

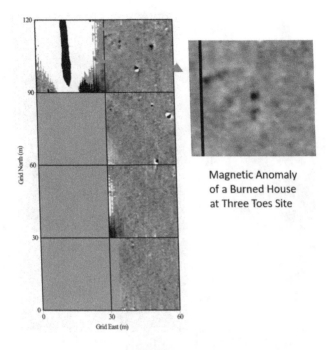

Magnetic Anomaly
of a Burned House
at Three Toes Site

Figure 15: A magnetometer map showing a buried pit-house anomaly at the Three Toes site. The image on the left covers an area measuring 120 meters north–south by 60 meters east–west, and the bold black line at upper left is a buried petroleum pipeline. The closeup section covers an area of about 16 x 16 meters and shows a distinctive magnetic signature. Archaeological testing has confirmed that this location is another burned pit-house. Map by David Maki.

teach us. As we dug test units in areas away from the hearth, things got weird. We were perplexed because we couldn't see the house floor, even though we knew it had once been there.

At Hank's and Drover's Houses, the floor was baked so hard that a trained monkey could have troweled down and identified the floor surface. But Pete's House didn't burn, and we couldn't find the floor! We began to feel like a bunch of untrained monkeys.

a

b

Figure 16a, b: Remote sensing surveys at West Pasture sites. (a) Chet Walker conducting a proton magnetometer survey. (b) Tiffany Osburn conducting a ground-penetrating radar survey with archaeological excavations at Drover's House in the background. Chet and Tiffany are both specialists in geophysical surveying. Photographs by Doug Boyd.

Two things happened that helped us redeem our status as good Texas archaeologists. First, using his best excavation skills and troweling slowly, Joe Rogers began to find artifacts that were lying horizontally at the same level. It started with a flint flake here and a bone fragment there. The pattern became more predictable, and we realized that Joe was finding artifacts left behind on the house floor, even though we couldn't see any sediment change to define the floor itself.

The second thing occurred when we dug a trench five meters long to create a cross-section of the pit-house. Although we still couldn't identify the floor level when we first dug the trench at midday, Charles Frederick insisted on waiting to examine the profile when the lighting was right.

Late in the day, when the east wall of the trench was illuminated in the soft light of sundown, the invisible house floor popped out. It was there the whole time. We just hadn't been able to see it.

Chapter 19
The Etched Rib

JOHN: Another discovery at Three Toes came our way in 2013 when a pipeline crew cut a ditch on the south end of West Pasture. Wilkens had chosen their route through an area where we had never found cultural material on the surface and where he assumed no sites existed.

Even so, he asked the foreman to report any material that might show up. The gentleman was kind enough to call when he saw bones in the ditch, and he shut down the operation for several days.

Wilkens flew into action and assembled a crew for a salvage excavation. Charles Frederick dropped what he was doing and drove up from Dublin. Joe Rogers came from Hereford, and Benny and Gina Roberts came from a dig in South Texas. Nikki Georgacakis flew up from San Antonio and helped Kris prepare good meals for the crew.

We found a large feature that appeared to be an unburned pit-house and several trash pits nearby that were rich with material, including a semi-precious stone (amethyst), a large, hafted flint knife, and a rib bone with a number of lines etched across its flat surface.

When I first saw that bone, I thought, "That looks almost like writing." I took a picture of it, and we continued with the excavation. The rib went into an artifact bag, and I forgot about it.

Six years later, I ran across the photo and, again, it looked very unusual—very unique. I asked Wilkens about it. He had cleaned it up, applied a clear preservative solution to keep it from breaking apart, and filed it away in a box of artifacts. I borrowed it and took it home for closer inspection.

It was not an entire rib, just a fragment approximately three-and-a-half inches long and three-quarters of an inch wide. It appeared too small to be the rib of a bison and too thick to be human. Wilkens thought it might be a deer rib. The lines were deep, straight, and carefully made. I counted twenty lines up to the point where the bone had broken off. The original unbroken rib could have contained more lines.

I hit the books and found a dozen references to notched ribs and incised ribs that had been reported at Plains Village sites in the Texas and Oklahoma Panhandles, western Oklahoma, and southeastern Colorado. They were variously described as a bone rasp, a musical rasp, and a gaming piece.

Our specimen showed no evidence of polish or wear on the surface, so that seemed to rule out any kind of scraping or musical function. A gaming piece? That might be as reasonable a guess as any.

When you're trying to interpret a culture seven centuries old you have to do some guessing, and I'll add my guess to the discussion. I'm inclined toward the idea that our etched rib was a counting device. The user was keeping a record of something and the commodity that comes to mind is *time*. I think it might have been some type of calendar device.

Ancient cultures the world over were very interested in keeping track of time. The Aztecs, Mayans, and Incas kept track of time using the sun, and so did the ancient Hebrews. The Egyptians and Mesopotamians and the Indus River civilizations followed the movements of the stars, planets, and moon. The Celts tracked time from sunset to sunrise, and the Egyptians as well as the Chinese tracked time on candles and water clocks. In North America, the Mound Builders of the Mississippi Valley, the Cherokee, and the Anasazi each had their own unique time-keeping systems. Why not the people in West Pasture?

The most obvious clock they had was the sun cycles of day and night, but they had another in the moon. Our fragment had twenty lines and was broken off on one end. Nine more lines would have given the approximate number of days in a lunar cycle: 29. Nine-and-a-half lines would have been even closer to the actual number, 29.53.

A report from the Landergin Mesa site west of Amarillo contained a drawing of an etched rib similar to ours. It showed 26 lines and was broken off on one end. It could have had 29 lines or 29.5. A stem of grass placed in a groove each day would have given Plains Village people a simple way of tracking lunar cycles.

We moderns tend to view the moon as the place where NASA astronauts planted the American flag in 1969: a lifeless chunk of rock that circles the earth. Pre-scientific cultures were aware of the moon as a force that had a real and even profound impact on their lives. When you stop and think, it does make sense.

Consider the force the moon's gravity exerts on the earth's oceans, tugging millions of tons of seawater into waves that crash onto beaches every night. A force that can move ocean water surely affects fluids in the human body, right down to each individual cell, including brain cells, and maybe each individual strand of DNA.

The words *lunacy* and *lunatic* originated at a time when most people believed that *la luna*, the moon, influenced human behavior. Maybe they were right, and maybe it still does.

> I have a friend whose wife has difficulty sleeping during a full moon.

> Schoolteachers cite the different behavior they observe in children during a full moon.

> Law enforcement officers mention an increase in violence during a full moon.

> Doctors and nurses who work in mental hospitals report changes in patient behavior during a full moon.

> Some scientists believe that conception rates in humans are influenced by the phases of the moon.

> Astrology has always argued that personality is partly shaped by heavenly bodies. Isaac Newton, perhaps the greatest scientist who ever lived, took astrology very seriously.

If the moon influences human behavior, it must affect plants and animals too. Why would it not? Our great-grandparents thought it did. They worked cattle and planted gardens by the "sign of the moon." Fishermen predicted the success of the catch by the sign of the moon.

It wouldn't be unreasonable to suppose that West Pasture people tracked lunar cycles to manage crops and hunting. Who knows, bison and deer might behave differently in different phases of the moon. We moderns tend to view that belief as superstition, but it could be a type of knowledge we have lost in exchange for cellular phones and washing machines.

If the etched rib served as a calendar, it would be the closest thing we've found to a written language . . . and while we're speculating, we might as well consider that possibility too. Most of us who dabble in archaeology assume that prehistoric people on the Southern Plains had no written language but suppose they did . . . and we don't recognize it.

Chinese writing consists of straight lines, curved lines, dots, and circles that have no meaning to us. Ancient Egyptians wrote with hieroglyphs and pictures that, without the Rosetta Stone, we wouldn't understand.

Cuneiform, the script of ancient Mesopotamia, was made up of wedge-shaped impressions stamped into damp clay. Those marks mean nothing to us, but 5,000 years ago, the oldest piece of literature known to mankind—the *Epic of Gilgamesh*—was recorded in cuneiform script.

At the same time people were living in West Pasture, the residents of Ireland had an alphabet of their own called *ogham*. The writing survives today as a series of slash marks on tall standing stones. Certain combinations gave consonants and others gave vowels. It was an awkward system, but it produced words and sentences.

It's hard to imagine that twenty straight lines etched onto a rib bone could mean anything beyond what we see, but it's something to ponder. The lines on our bone are not all the same length and the spaces between them are not a uniform width. Maybe those subtle differences had a meaning that isn't obvious to us any more than the difference between our letter **T** and number **7** would have been obvious to prehistoric residents of West Pasture.

My first impression when I saw the rib was that those lines were more than just lines. They *meant* something. First impressions are based on intuition—sometimes they're wrong, but sometimes they can also be right. In the age of science, we have a tendency to talk ourselves out of first impressions.

I can't prove any of my speculations, of course, and I doubt that other researchers can prove theirs. We're all groping to understand ancient people who didn't leave much evidence for us to study.

DOUG: The finding of the etched deer rib got all of us excited, and Erickson was especially curious to know its significance. I could sense his disappointment when we had to conclude that we didn't know for sure. Archaeology is like that sometimes. I could have made up a good story that sounded believable, but Erickson would have probably caught me and called my bluff.

It is unlikely that engraved markings on the etched bone are random scratches or merely doodling with a flint flake on bone. The markings did have some meaning to the person who created them, and those symbols could be read and understood by others in his or her group.

Archaeologists often use ethnographic analogy to help interpret things that we find. An analogy is a comparison, and ethnography refers to historic-period observations made about one culture by another culture.

When the Spanish came into the Southwest, they observed and recorded lots of details about the Pueblo Indians that they encountered. An ethnographic analogy is when we use those historic observations of Puebloan artifacts and behaviors to help us interpret the lives of pre-historic Pueblo Indians or other Native American groups mentioned in the documents.

If I were asked to interpret what those engraved lines meant, I would use the ethnographic analogy concept and suggest that the etched bone from Three Toes was some

Figure 17: Photograph of the etched rib found at the Three Toes site. Who made the unusual markings on this bone, and what do they mean? Photograph by Doug Wilkens.

type of counting device or calendar as John suggests, or it might have been a gaming piece.

Playing games is a human endeavor, and people in every culture around the world have played games that require specialized objects that were adorned with meaningful symbols. Think of modern dice and dominoes as an analogy for prehistoric gaming pieces. How many different games can you play with a simple cube or rectangle covered with dots symbolizing numbers?

Chapter 20
Water and Fire
Educator's Guide reference: Activity 7

J OHN: When we began our West Pasture research, the nearest watercourse, West Fork of Pickett Ranch Creek, was bone dry and probably had been for half a century or more. The nearest flowing spring lay three-quarters of a mile to the north at Indian Springs.

We can be certain that prehistoric residents would not have settled in an area that lacked a reliable source of drinking water, so where did they get it?

We must assume that the tributary stream we see today is not the same as the one that existed in AD 1300. We know the region experienced periods of disastrous drought after West Pasture people abandoned their homes (remember, Hank's House was buried under seven feet of blown sand), so we can assume that springs dried up and were smothered by topsoil.

We also know that European settlement brought many changes that diminished the flow of springs in the Canadian River Valley. The most obvious cause was the rise of irrigation agriculture that has drawn down the level of the Ogallala Aquifer and decreased spring flow.

Another change, not so obvious, is that European settlement altered the natural ecology of the prairie, specifically as it related to fire. Beginning around 1880, Anglo settlers brought European ideas about the ownership of land that encouraged the building of fences, houses, barns, schools, churches, and towns, and owners went to great lengths to keep them from burning. Fire was viewed as the enemy of civilization, and every little town had a volunteer fire brigade that turned out to fight fires on the prairie.

Settlers planted trees to soften the barren landscape and chose varieties that could survive in a semi-arid climate: the native one-seed juniper and red cedar and the non-native salt cedar and Russian olive. Those hardy trees survived, all right. Their seeds scattered and took root, and they have prospered to the point of becoming a plague of feral brush.

Cattle ranching contributed to the spread of mesquite into the Panhandle. Mesquite beans passed through the digestive systems of the cattle and sprouted in ground that had been disturbed by overgrazing. Over the past century and a half, the mesquite line has crept northward into the Canadian River Valley.

The rapid spread of trees, both native and non-native, was a direct result of fire suppression, and it has affected spring flow. One juniper tree pulling thirty gallons of water per day from the soil hardly makes an impression, but when ten thousand junipers in the watershed pull three hundred thousand gallons per day, springs stop flowing and creeks dry up.

The irony is that our suppression of natural fire has made us vulnerable to wildfires that are so big, we can't stop them. When the wind blows 50 to 60 miles per hour and the relative humidity drops to 10 percent, one little spark can turn dry grass and feral brush into a megafire, the National Weather Service's term for a wildfire that burns 100,000 acres or more.

That was the kind of inferno that struck us on March 6, 2017, when three massive prairie fires swept across Texas, Oklahoma, and Kansas, burning 1.2 million acres of grassland in one blustery afternoon. Our ranch was in the path of the 318,000-acre Perryton Fire. We lost our home, a guest house, my writing office, and 90 percent of our pastures. I lost my entire library of Southern Plains archaeology—every book and article.

In the months and years that followed, I had the opportunity to observe the fire's impact on our range conditions, and for the most part, it was very positive. The fire cleaned out yucca, cactus, and other invader species and, more important, it killed tens of thousands of water-sucking junipers and mesquites.

Within months, I observed an increase in the flow of existing springs and found new spring pools in places where we had never seen them. That included West Fork of Pickett Ranch Creek, the tributary that ran through our village sites in West Pasture.

We can suppose that the 2017 fire restored the prairie to something close to what it looked like in AD 1300. If, in the fourteenth century, the prairie burned on a regular basis—fire experts assure us that it did—the watershed would have been swept clean of junk brush with only a few pockets of cedar surviving in protected canyons.

After centuries of regular burning, the water table would have been close enough to the surface to support a line of spring pools a mile or more in length, or even a flowing stream. That was surely the source of water for our village residents in West Pasture.

It wouldn't be outrageous to suppose that they used fire as a management tool. They might have used controlled burning to protect and manage groves of large cedar that were, in effect, the lumberyard for their houses. They also might have understood the subtle relationship between fire and water and used burning as a tool for managing their water supply—keeping springs active and alive.

I doubt that we could prove or disprove this hypothesis by the archaeological record (what evidence would remain after seven hundred years?), but it would be a mistake to underestimate the intelligence of these people. Their very survival in a harsh environment is proof of an intelligence we must admire.

DOUG: There is ample ethnographic and archaeological evidence that Native Americans sometimes used fire as a tool. Historically, Native Americans living in the Great Plains took advantage of the natural wildfires caused by thunderstorms, and they also started fires when it suited them. The evidence indicates the native peoples started fires to create better grasslands for attracting bison, and they also started fires as a means of driving bison for hunting purposes.

In some places in Montana, they started prairie fires to move bison herds into their drive lines, which were marked by piles of rocks. As the animals fled the fire, people would jump out from behind the drive-line rock piles, scaring the animals into a frenzied run and herding them right over a steep cliff.

Archaeologists have known about these buffalo-jump kill sites for a long time because this type of communal hunting is well documented in prehistoric and historic times. Only within the last few decades have we begun to realize that anthropogenic (man-made) fires played a prominent role in bison hunting far back into prehistory.

Plains Villagers in the Texas Panhandle may have set fires occasionally because they knew fire was beneficial for

a

b

Figure 18a, b: Photographs of John and Kris Erickson's ranch house before (a) and after (b) the devastating Perryton Fire of March 2017. Fire has long been an important part of the grassland ecology on the Great Plains, whether the prairie fires started naturally or were intentionally set by humans to manage the landscape. Unfortunately, modern wildfires can be very destructive to humans. Photographs by Doug Boyd (a) and Doug Wilkens (b).

the grassland prairies that bison like. They may have set fires to manipulate the movements of buffalo herds or even as part of their buffalo-hunting strategy.

We haven't found a Plains Village buffalo-jump kill site in the Texas Panhandle yet, but there are probably some of them out there.

Chapter 21
Fire Protection
Educator's Guide reference: Activity 7

J **OHN:** Because I lost my home in the 2017 fire, I was curious about how West Pasture people coexisted with this ever-present force of nature. Part of the answer might be that the prairie in AD 1300 was less flammable than the one we saw in 2017. Bison herds kept the grass grazed short and regular lightning-caused fires kept the prairie free of woody vegetation. Also, we can assume that prehistoric people used controlled burns to keep their living areas free of tall grass and brush.

Our research of structures in West Pasture provides another answer: our people lived in dirt-covered pit-houses, *earth lodges*, that were immune to fire from the outside.

For decades, artist depictions and museum dioramas of Plains Village structures in the Panhandle have shown houses with roofs made of thatched grass. That has been the accepted view, but it sidesteps the question of how a grass roof could withstand the constant, tearing lateral force of Panhandle wind. A house with a grass roof would have been a sitting duck for a prairie fire and a death trap for anyone inside. The wildfires of 2017 made the model even less plausible.

The earth lodge has long been known to be a common house type in Upper Republican sites in Kansas, Nebraska, and the Dakotas, but most researchers doubted that they ever appeared in our area. The closest earth lodges to us (that we knew about) were reported near Pratt, Kansas, and Limon, Colorado. Archaeologists had been studying Plains Village ruins in the Panhandle for more than a century, and nobody had ever found an earth lodge or had even suspected one might exist. In professional circles, it was a controversial hypothesis.

For our team, it wasn't a hypothesis. We had the evidence.

Chapter 22

A Closer Look at Drover's House

Educator's Guide reference: Activity 7

J OHN: In 2004, we began excavating Drover's House, about half a mile from Hank's House. From the surface evidence Doug Boyd and Doug Wilkens knew that it would be a burned structure, like Hank's. They were alert to the possibility that it might contain a layer of burned soil that would indicate an earthen roof. Boyd designed the excavation to look for that feature and added geoarchaeologist Charles Frederick to the team.

Charles holds a doctorate in geomorphology. He had analyzed pit-houses in many locations in Europe, Mexico, and the US. He recorded the evidence from Drover's House in meticulous detail and was convinced it was an earth lodge, intentionally burned from the inside.

The intense burning of Drover's House produced hundreds of pounds of ceiling plaster and burned daub: a mix of mud and grass that had been heated to the consistency of pottery. Those daub specimens contained astonishing images of small branches, grass, big framing members, rope lashings made of vegetable fiber, and even the handprints and fingerprints of the builders.

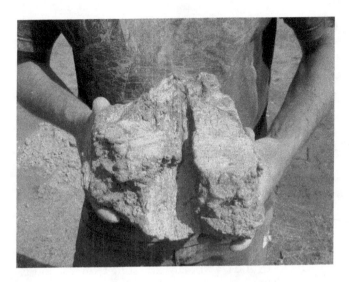

Figure 19: Archaeologist holding a large piece of burned daub recovered from Drover's House. Burned daub represents the clay material in the roof superstructure and got intensively heated when the lodge burned down. The fire was so hot that the baked clay has a ceramic-like consistency, thus preserving it for archaeologists to find. Photograph by Doug Boyd.

Doug Wilkens took it upon himself to study boxes of fire-hardened daub, a three-year project that involved measuring, weighing, photographing, and analyzing every specimen, and determining its location within the structure.

He worked with Charles Frederick, architects, and a structural engineer to create a blueprint and reverse-engineer a house model with precise measurements based on data from Drover's House. Using stress tables applied to wood and soil samples taken from the ranch, the architects and engineer proved that a structure made of local materials could support the considerable weight of an earthen roof, even when it was saturated with water.

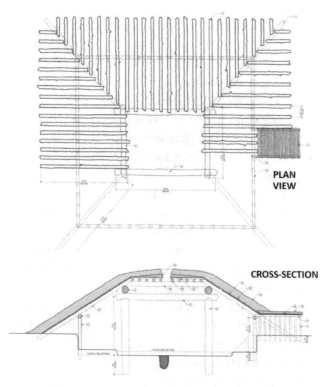

PLAN VIEW

CROSS-SECTION

**Reconstruction of Drover's House Based on
Reverse Engineering Principles**

Figure 20: Model of Drover's House earth lodge based on reverse engineering. These drawings depict how the lodge walls and roof superstructure were probably designed. Engineering and architectural analyses by Michael Westbrook and Ryan Wilkens. Computer drafted images by Ryan and Doug Wilkens.

Again, the mass of evidence shouted that this was an earth lodge.

DOUG: From our work excavating the surviving one-half of Hank's House, we had learned a lot about digging in masses of burned daub and charred wood. It was there that we realized that most of what we were digging through to get to the floor was the remains of the roof.

When Erickson found Drover's House, we knew it was an amazing opportunity and we should investigate it the right way. It was a complete burned pit-house, and there would be more architectural evidence than there was in Hank's House.

We also knew that we could learn more from Drover's House if we used more rigorous excavation methods, mapped everything in greater detail, collected every scrap of burned daub (right down to fingernail-sized pieces), and paid more attention to documenting the earthen fill above the burned wood and daub layers.

We approached the investigation of Drover's House with the hypothesis that it was an earth lodge—a pit-house that once had a substantial earthen roof braced by a framework of wooden timbers supported by vertical posts. There were several dig sessions spread out over several years, but each one was organized to gather the various types of evidence that would be needed to prove—or disprove—our earthen roof hypothesis. This is why we needed Charles Frederick, a superstar geoarchaeologist.

Chapter 23

Were There Other Earth Lodges in the Panhandle?

Educator's Guide reference: Activity 7

J **OHN:** The Mowry Bluff site contained a burned rectangular pit-house with picket-post construction, four central posts, a covered entry, and a central fire pit. Excavators found ten inches of earth on top of a floor that was littered with well-fired daub, smooth on one side and with the other side holding impressions of sticks and grass. They concluded that it was an earth lodge.

The Mowry Bluff site was almost a mirror image of our structures at Hank and Drover, but it was located on a tributary of the Republican River . . . in Nebraska, where investigators *expected* to find an earth lodge.

Unless a house has burned, the evidence for a dirt-covered roof is hard to detect; it's nothing but a very subtle change in the color of the soil. If the team begins with the assumption that an earth lodge *can't* exist in the region, they're not likely to find evidence that disproves what they already believe to be solid fact. It is possible that our team had stumbled upon the only two earth lodges ever built in the Texas Panhandle, but it seems more likely that similar structures excavated in our region were not recognized as earth lodges.

In a typical excavation, the overburden, which is all the soil above the floor, is treated as an obstacle to the primary objective of reaching the floor, the living surface. That is where you find tools, arrow points, grinding stones, bone fragments, pottery, charred seeds, and datable charcoal.

The process of exposing the living surface is usually referred to as "chunking out." Volunteers use shovels or machinery to remove the overburden; then the archaeologists take over with a careful, controlled, documented excavation of the floor surface, using trowels, brushes, and dental tools.

The chunking-out method was typical of excavations in the past and remains a common practice today. It is valid when the overburden consists of soil that has blown or washed into the site, but it can destroy the most important evidence of an earth lodge: roof fall.

Roof fall is dirt that is more than dirt. It's an artifact that contains valuable information, like changes in color that indicate a disturbance of the soil or, in the case of a burned house, exposure to high temperature. Unless you're looking for it, and unless you're dealing with a burned house, you're not likely to find it.

Our team has not attempted to explain how an architectural style that is usually identified with later-period earth lodge builders in the Central and Northern Plains ended up in the Texas Panhandle, nor do we speculate about the cultural affiliation of the builders. We work with the evidence in our possession and let it speak for itself: around AD 1300, an as-yet-unidentified group of Plains Village people were building earth lodges in what is now northeastern Roberts County, Texas.

Were There Other Earth Lodges in the Panhandle?

It makes sense that prehistoric builders in West Pasture would have chosen the earth lodge design. The first Anglo settlers in the region adopted a similar design with their sod houses and half-dugouts. The earth lodge would have been perfectly adapted to the Plains environment, offering protection from summer heat and the wind-driven cold of winter. It would have also made them immune to the destruction of prairie fires.

DOUG: The end result of our archaeological investigations at Drover's House led us to one unmistakable conclusion: multiple lines of archaeological and engineering evidence demonstrated that Drover's House was indeed an earth lodge. Except for some very minor details, the architecture of Hank's House is the same as Drover's House. There is little doubt that Hank's House was also an earth lodge. That makes two definite earth lodges in the West Pasture.

We have tested two more burned pit-houses and three unburned pit-houses in the West Pasture. They are all the same kind and size of house as Hank's and Drover's Houses. We haven't excavated enough to prove that these other prehistoric houses were earth lodges, but the similarities are so striking that it would be hard to argue that they represent a different type of house construction.

Thus, it appears that the earth lodge was the house of choice for people living in the West Pasture community during the Plains Village period.

Let's take one more step back and look beyond the West Pasture. As Erickson mentioned earlier, picket-post houses have been investigated at other sites in the Texas Panhandle—at Cantonment Creek, Courson A, Chill Hill, Eastview, Long View, Footprint III, and Jack Allen. All of these houses could have been of earth lodge construction, but we will probably never know for sure because most of these houses were not burned and many were excavated several years ago before anyone paid much attention to the house fill. They didn't have geoarchaeologists analyzing the stratigraphic profiles and soil samples to see where house fill came from.

When the archaeologists worked at the Footprint site (now in the Lake Meredith area) in the 1960s, they dug three large rectangular houses they called Footprint I, Footprint II, and Footprint III. Only Footprint III had picket-post walls, while the others had rock foundations more typical of that area. The lead archaeologist, F. E. Green, made a very important observation when he wrote, "Upper walls of the large rectangular rooms must have been sufficiently strong to help support a roof of mud or clay-covered poles and brush and were probably occupied throughout the year." Green apparently recognized that the rectangular houses at the Footprint site were substantial structures with earthen roofs, although he didn't call them earth lodges.[1]

The Jack Allen house was completely excavated in 1969. Like the Hank and Drover houses, it got burned in a really hot fire, so its architectural details were beautifully preserved. In many ways, the Jack Allen house is a dead ringer for Hank's and Drover's Houses, and these sites are only about 50 miles apart. They all share many architectural similarities—charred wooden posts were still in place along the walls and in the four roof support postholes.

Back in 1969, there was no geoarchaeologist around to study the house fill inside the Jack Allen house. This will always leave a significant gap in the story. Fortunately,

---

1   F. E. Green, *Report on Archaeological Salvage in the Sanford Reservoir Area*, Panhandle Archaeological Society Publication no. 4, 109. Annotated by Christopher Lintz. The original report was published in 1967 by the Texas Technological College and the National Park Service.

the lead archaeologist, Jack Hughes, decided to save *all of the burned daub* found inside the house. This is amazing, because at most burned houses excavated more than 30 years ago in the Great Plains, no one kept the fired daub. They just didn't think it was important.

One of our West Pasture archaeological colleagues, Joe Rogers, got interested in this and decided to study the burned daub from the Jack Allen house. He spent a lot of time in the basement of the Panhandle-Plains Historical Museum conducting a detailed analysis of each and every piece of daub.

He and Wilkens reviewed all the site records and an unpublished site report draft that was written by Billy Harrison in the 1970s. The archaeological evidence makes a pretty strong case that the Jack Allen house was an earth lodge. Harrison himself speculated on this possibility. In his field notes from November 22, 1969, he wrote, "The profile along the south wall is very interesting as it shows that the house may have been mounded over with sod as a true earthen lodge."[2]

After many years of painstaking research, the West Pasture team had compiled the evidence needed to prove that there were earth lodges in the Texas Panhandle during the Plains Village period. The implication of this is pretty important, because the closest spots in the Great Plains where similar prehistoric earth lodges are recognized are in south-central Kansas and southern Nebraska.

---

2   Handwritten field notes by Billy R. Harrison on the excavations at the Jack Allen site, November 22, 1969. Original document on file at the Panhandle-Plains Historical Museum, West Texas A&M University, Canyon, TX.

Chapter 24

Unanswered Questions

Educator's Guide reference: Activity 8

JOHN: If I had the opportunity to spend an evening around a fire with West Pasture people, I think I would like them . . . and their kids and their dogs. I would want to hear their stories. I would bombard them with questions.

How did they cut down those big cedar trees that served as central support posts in their houses?

What kind of chopping tool did they use? We haven't found any tools that would chop down a big tree.

How did they lug those logs a mile from the canyons to the house site? I have cut down some of those big trees with a chainsaw and they must weigh between 1,000 and 2,000 pounds.

Did they have a system for keeping track of time? Did they have a calendar?

How much did they know about the movement of sun, moon, and stars?

Did they eat grasshoppers? I'll bet they did. Grasshoppers would have been a ready source of protein and the kids could have done the hunting.

Where did they find clay for making pots?

How long did it take them to learn how to make a perfect Washita point?

DOUG: Like Erickson, I would love to spend one evening in a campfire chat with the West Pasture folks. The first questions I would ask are: Who are your relatives? Where did your people live before they came to settle in the area we call West Pasture?

When I was just starting out in my Panhandle archaeological studies, one of the first things I learned about the Plains Villagers is they seemed to appear suddenly in the Texas Panhandle, but we didn't know where they came from. I learned that there were two main theories to explain this.

Theory #1 says that the local Plains Woodland people evolved—meaning they changed lifestyles—into the Plains Villagers because they adopted farming and buffalo hunting at the same time. Climatic evidence indicates that rapid shifts in rainfall patterns favored shortgrass prairies in the Southern Plains, and these ideal conditions allowed the buffalo populations to suddenly explode. Archaeological evidence indicates that the buffalo herds did increase dramatically at this time.

Theory #2 says that the people came from somewhere else and migrated into the Texas Panhandle. Most evidence seems to suggest that the Plains Villagers in the Panhandle came from somewhere in the north, and that climate changes caused them to migrate southward, perhaps to be closer to expanding buffalo herds.

The problem with Theory #1 is that we have fairly scant archaeological evidence for the Plains Woodland period, and we certainly don't have enough evidence to prove that they evolved into the Plains Village peoples.

Theory #2 seems to apply fairly well to the eastern Texas Panhandle, especially given the archaeological evidence we see coming out of the West Pasture and the Buried City area. Theory #2 doesn't seem as viable for the central and western Texas Panhandle, where much of the influence seems to be coming from southeastern Colorado and the Puebloan cultures to the west.

If I were to guess, I'd say both theories may be partly true. I think the Plains Woodland peoples in the Panhandle did adopt farming and bison hunting at the same time that new groups of people were migrating in from the north. The local Plains Villagers may well be a mixture, with some villages being the original Panhandlers and others being the newcomers. This is the best explanation I can see to explain the evidence we have right now.

Chapter 25

Gardens and Predators

J OHN: Here's a question I've thought about many times. Farming was a very serious business for our West Pasture people, maybe a matter of life and death. How did they protect their crops from predator animals?

Over the years, Kris and I have had a lot of experience trying to raise a garden in the same climate and on the same land as the West Pasture villagers. One of the things we have learned about gardening is that in the summertime, anything *green* draws a crowd, and the nicer the garden, the bigger the crowd: raccoons, coyotes, rabbits, and deer.

Coons are very intelligent and are the worst offenders. Once they have found a food source, they keep coming back. They work at night, and you never see them during the daylight hours. They don't wait for the crop to ripen and mature—they dig up the seeds as soon as you plant them. You replant and they come back. If you're fortunate enough to nurse your crop along to harvest, the coons will get there first and harvest it for you.

One of our neighbors on the Canadian River planted a vineyard. The first year his vines produced a crop, the coons totally stripped the vines. After several failed attempts to keep them out, he finally hit upon a system that worked: a six-foot fence of woven wire, chicken wire buried in a ditch to prevent burrowing, and two electric wires hooked up to 110-volt house current. Only then was he able to harvest his grapes.

West Pasture people didn't have electric fences, and I find it hard to believe they could have protected their crops by hunting and trapping. Maybe they camped out in their fields, perhaps using children for the task. The presence of human scent might have been enough to keep animals away for a while, but I suspect that during the course of a four-month growing season, the animals would have figured out the game and lost their fear, the same way crows lose their fear of a scarecrow.

Maybe the children stayed awake all night, beating sticks together and burning campfires, but again it seems that over a four-month growing season, the advantage would have tilted toward animals that were always hungry and didn't sleep at night. Children get tired and lose focus, and an entire crop could have been lost in one careless night.

The most logical answer I can come up with is that they used dogs. Maybe they tethered them in garden plots so they could bark the alarm, or maybe they trained them to patrol the gardens and kill animals that encroached. Such dogs would have been formidable fighters, because coyotes often run in packs and coons are dangerous adversaries.

Dog bones and dog burials have been reported in North American sites as far back as 10,000 years ago. Prehistoric people used them as companions, beasts of burden, and guards. In hard times, they ate them.

The problem with my dog theory is that, so far, we have found no evidence of dog bones or dog burials in our sites.

Phooey.

Figure 21: Doug Wilkens and John Erickson examine an underground storage pit found near Hank's House. Plains Village people dug pits and used them to store surplus crop foods like corn, beans, and squash. This one was fairly small, and it appeared as gray soil inside a bell-shaped pit that was dug into the light brown sandy soil. Photograph by Doug Boyd.

DOUG: Farming and dogs are both important research topics for all of us West Pasture archaeologists. John is right that farming was a serious business for the Plains Village people. Once they made a commitment to growing corn and other crops, people had to have semi-permanent villages near their fields.

When it was nearing harvest time, people had to defend their precious plants from raiders or there would be no food left for them. In many areas of the world, the beginning of farming meant that people began to build more permanent houses and live together in villages.

We have another important line of archaeological evidence in the West Pasture that indicates how important farming was to these folks. At every location where we find

Plains Village houses, we also find underground storage pits. Some were large cylindrical pits with a capacity of fifty bushels or more, but most of them were smaller bell-shaped pits that could hold fifteen to thirty bushels of dried crop foods.

The finding of underground storage pits is significant because it proves that the West Pasture people produced a surplus of crops so that they could store them for use during the winter months when food was scarce.

Now what about dogs? A guy who writes books about a cowdog would naturally spend some time thinking about whether the prehistoric people who lived on his ranch had village dogs, right? I shouldn't have been surprised one evening when our West Pasture group was sitting on Erickson's porch and he asked us, "Where were the dogs?"

The question caught me completely off guard because it hadn't yet crossed my mind. Duh! It was a great question.

There is ample evidence that many historic and pre-historic Native American cultures had dogs. When the Spanish explorer Coronado came through the Texas Panhandle in 1541, he saw the Querechos (probably bands of Apache peoples) using big dogs to pull sleds loaded down with their tipis and belongings. The French called these conveyances *travois*, and this word (which can be singular or plural) is now used to describe a triangular sled consisting of two poles supporting a platform that could be loaded with supplies and dragged by a dog or a horse. After Native Americans got horses, they could use horses and dogs to pull travois. In pre-horse times, dogs were only logical choice to help people carry their belongings using a travois.

Think about this for a moment. What if Hank the Cowdog had lived in Plains Village times? Would he have

Figure 22. A dog harnessed to a travois, a type of sled consisting of two poles used to support a platform that could be dragged by a dog or a horse. This image is a section from an 1844 painting by western artist Karl Bodmer. It depicts people of the Assiniboine nation in the northern Great Plains. The painting is from US Library of Congress and is in the public domain. https://commons.wikimedia.org/wiki/File:Dog_with_travois._Detail_of_Karl_Bodmer_painting_-_A_Skin_Lodge_of_an_Assiniboin_Chief.jpg

been harnessed up to a travois to help his people carry heavy loads? Would his self-proclaimed title have been "Head of Village Transportation"?

Archaeological remains of domesticated dogs—which are quite different than their wolf ancestors—have been found in many places across North America going back at least 9,000 years. Most archaeologists believe that dogs were traveling with the waves of Native American groups that came across the Bering Strait and into North America more than 12,000 years ago. The relationship between dogs and humans is ancient.

Archaeologically, the dog remains that are found in most village settings are often whole skeletons that were buried in graves just like people. This suggests that dogs were not just seen as work animals or guard dogs; they were treated as pets and family members.

Like Erickson, I believe the West Pasture people had dogs. I also think it is just a matter of time until we find the archaeological evidence to prove it.

Chapter 26
Trade

J OHN: I've also wondered about the nonlocal materials we've found in our sites. They indicate that some kind of trading network existed in AD 1300. Our people traded something they produced locally for goods they had to obtain through bartering.

> **Obsidian**: Many of our sites contain small amounts of this black volcanic glass that they used for making high-quality points and cutting tools. It is a nonlocal material, and geochemists have traced obsidian artifacts found in the Southern Plains to Idaho and the Jemez Mountains of New Mexico.
>
> *Olivella* **shell**: These little shells were used as beads and originated in ocean water, so they were trade items that came from a long distance and must have been highly prized.
>
> **Southwestern pottery**: We have recovered a small number of pottery sherds that are very different from locally made ceramics and appear to have been crafted by the expert Pueblo potters in New Mexico. The Southwestern sherds are thin, hard, painted, and glazed. When I find one of these fragments, I wish I had found the entire vessel. It must have been a beautiful creation.

> **Nonlocal chert**: "Chert" is a word archaeologists use for certain types of rock used to produce arrow points, knives, drills, and scrapers. Flint is a type of chert. We have found several types of nonlocal chert that must have come through trade: Niobrara jasper from Nebraska, Dakota quartzite from the Black Mesa area in northwest Oklahoma or northeastern New Mexico, and Tecovas jasper from the northwestern Texas Panhandle or the Caprock Canyonland to the south.

What did our folks have to trade? Probably products derived from bison: dried meat, hides, horns, and perhaps tools made of bone.

For me, the big question is, how did people who had no wheeled vehicles or beasts of burden maintain trading relationships across hundreds of miles of semi-arid terrain? How did West Pasture people lug buffalo hides four hundred miles to Pueblo villages in New Mexico, then transport loads of bulky, fragile pots from the Rio Grande River to an isolated hamlet in the Canadian River Valley?

Perhaps the trade occurred in steps, with several cultural groups involved along the way. Maybe they used dogs as beasts of burden but, once again, we have no dog bones to prove it.

It's easy to state the obvious (they were conducting trade and bringing in nonlocal materials) but hard to figure out exactly how they did it. At some point, you have to explain trade as an exchange of calories: somehow the reward must equal or exceed the effort. My best attempts to figure this out have failed.

One last observation on trade. The most common chert we find on the ranch is Alibates flint. There were two sources for it: river cobbles that showed up in local gravel deposits and the Alibates flint quarries north of Amarillo.

The quarries were located fifty or sixty miles upriver from West Pasture, where Antelope Creek people mined it in chunks and slabs.

Alibates flint is a trade item you would expect to find in our West Pasture sites. It was probably the best tool-making material in North America, and it has been found in sites a thousand miles away, yet the tools we find in our sites appear to have been made from small river cobbles, not slabs that came out of a quarry. The tools we've recovered are small and worn-out.

If our people had been trading for Alibates flint, we would find more and larger tools (axes and four-bladed knives) as well as caches of preforms, blanks, and chunks of flint buried in pits, but that has not been the case. Our people were making tools with material they found close by and using their tools until there wasn't much left of them.

Why would they *not* have traded with the Antelope Creek communities that were the custodians of the Alibates quarries and located not far from West Pasture? Excavation material from Buried City sites shows the same thing: they weren't trading with the people who controlled the Alibates flint quarries.

Maybe our folks weren't related to Antelope Creek by blood or culture. Maybe they didn't get along well. Once again, we can only guess.

DOUG: Archaeologists spend a lot of time studying "prehistoric exchange systems." Basically, we want to know who was trading what, to whom, and when. We try to track the movements of people and ideas across the landscape by studying material remains.

In most Plains Village sites in the Texas Panhandle, we find artifacts that are nonlocal or exotic, and we know that they were brought in from faraway places. We use all sorts of scientific analysis methods to find out where the objects came from so that we can begin to understand how they got into the Panhandle sites.

Let's look at the obsidian artifacts and marine shells we find in the Texas Panhandle.

Obsidian is a black glass created by volcanic eruptions, and a chemical analysis can link each piece of obsidian to a specific volcanic area (there are none in the Texas Panhandle). Most of the obsidian found in Panhandle Plains Village sites came from the Jemez Mountains in northern New Mexico. It was picked up first by the local Pueblo Indians and then traded to various groups of people living on the plains.

If you dig enough at any Panhandle village site, you will likely find one or more shell beads of a genus called *Olivella*. We know that these shells were modified so that they could be strung together and worn as bracelets and necklaces. These shells originated in the Pacific Ocean. They were traded from one group to another, passing through the hands of the Pueblo Indians before they ended up at least 800 miles away in the Texas Panhandle!

When archaeologists want to study prehistoric exchange systems, the other artifact we love to examine is pottery. We find a lot of broken pottery sherds in our West Pasture digs, and most of it is the typical plain cordmarked variety that is common in Plains Village sites all over the Panhandle.

We also find quite a bit of pottery that we call decorated cordmarked and some decorated pottery that is not cordmarked. These decorated types of pottery are rare in the central and western Texas Panhandle village sites, but they are fairly common in the eastern Texas Panhandle village sites, especially in the West Pasture and the Buried

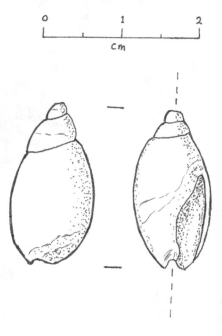

Figure 23. An *Olivella* bead made from a small seashell that came from the Pacific Coast. These beads were strung together in bundles and were traded from group to group until they were finally acquired by Plains Village people living in the Texas Panhandle. Drawing by Doug Boyd.

City sites.

The fact that we find a lot of decorated pottery in West Pasture isn't a trivial observation. We see lots of pottery that has impressed, or incised, decorations added to the shoulder, neck, and rim areas, and fingernail impressions around pot rims are especially common.

Most of these decorative styles we see in West Pasture and other eastern Panhandle sites match the pottery styles found in the Oklahoma Panhandle, southern Kansas, and even Nebraska. Here we must ask ourselves: Were the pots

Figure 24a, b, c, d, e. Pottery sherds found at West Pasture sites on the M-Cross Ranch. (a) and (b) are "cordmarked" sherds that are commonly found in Plains Village sites; (c) is a cordmarked sherd with a flattened rim and fingernail impressions; (d) is a cordmarked pot with an engraved "chevron" pattern added; (e) is a plainware (no cordmarking) that has fingernail impressions around the rim. Photographs by Doug Wilkens.

being traded? Or were the decorative ideas being transferred from one group to another?

We still have a lot of work to do to determine if any of the decorated pots we find in West Pasture were actually made at sites far to the north or if the pots were made in West Pasture using decorative ideas that came from the north.

Either way, the pottery is telling us the same thing that our earth lodges are telling us. The West Pasture people interacted with Plains Village cultures to the north, and they may have been related to those people.

This is not what we expected to learn when we began this research years ago. This is, as we say, "Typical West Pasture."

Chapter 27

Collectors, Landowners, and Archaeologists

J OHN: A lot of years have passed since I was a Boy Scout, picking up arrowheads at Black Mesa and storing them in my sock drawer. I am now a landowner as well as an amateur collector and have worked beside professional archaeologists. Maybe we should conclude with some thoughts on how collectors, landowners, and archaeologists can work together.

Collectors: As I said in the beginning, collecting arrowheads is not the same as collecting seashells on a beach. We have an inexhaustible supply of seashells, but prehistoric artifacts are a finite resource. Once we pick them up, they're gone and out of their original context. Anyone who collects artifacts should abide by a few simple rules:

Learn to respect ancient people and ancient knowledge.

Do some reading on local archaeology and share your literature with other collectors. And with landowners.

Keep a record of the "provenance" of an artifact—where it came from.

Organize artifact collections by site location.

Collect only objects that appear on the surface.

Leave non-collectible debris in place. It marks the spot as a habitation site.

Don't dig into a site. It destroys valuable information.

Landowners: Landowners should inform themselves on local history and archaeology and think of themselves as stewards of a precious resource. They should seek out people in the area who have an interest in archaeology and who might be willing to participate in a disciplined exploration of sites: people affiliated with universities, museums, historical groups, or state archaeological societies.

Archaeologists: Any professional archaeologist is likely to have mixed feelings about collectors. On the one hand, amateurs sometimes appear uninformed and undisciplined. They disturb the context of an ancient object and, in the worst cases, chop and hack their way into valuable sites, destroying all information they might have contained. On the other hand, an archaeologist can benefit from the curiosity and energy of amateurs who know their country and can discover sites a professional might never find. If an amateur keeps good records, an archaeologist can glance at a bag of artifacts and get a pretty accurate idea of who made them, and when.

When collectors acquire knowledge and discipline from professionals, they can make a contribution to the effort, serving the same function I have provided for our team: finding sites and keeping a record of surface evidence. Our work in West Pasture has been a joint effort between me as the landowner and other amateurs and professionals. It has been a very rewarding experience for all of us.

DOUG: In many states, lots of land is owned or controlled by public entities (federal government, state government, counties, cities, river authorities, and other types of political subdivisions). This is not true of Texas, where 95 percent of the land is privately owned.

When cultural resources (which includes all types of archaeological and historical sites) occur on public lands, they are protected by various state and federal laws, while the cultural resources occurring on private lands are not. In Texas, it is an indisputable fact that the future of our past is in private hands.

This is, I have found over my four decades working as a professional archaeologist, generally a very good thing for the state of Texas. Most landowners are great stewards of their land, and they don't participate in or condone the destruction of archeological resources.

The West Pasture archaeological project is a wonderful example of collaboration between professional archaeologists, avocational archaeologists, and private landowners. When I first set foot onto the M-Cross Ranch twenty years ago, I had no idea what adventures lay ahead. The opportunity to investigate important Plains Village sites like the ones in the West Pasture is rare indeed.

All of us who have volunteered time to excavate there are aware of this. While this archaeological journey has led us to many answers to questions we have asked about Texas Panhandle prehistory, it has also led us to many more questions that we cannot yet answer. In a nutshell, that is how archaeology works.

This book is not the end of the story for the West Pasture Archaeological Project. In fact, it is just the beginning. In order to continue our research in the West Pasture and to expand it beyond the ranch boundaries, we created a non-profit organization called Plains Archeological Research (PAR). PAR will provide us a way to seek funding to support our work, and this is important because doing good archaeology is expensive.

We still have much to do to complete the analyses of all the artifacts and samples we have collected. After we analyze our materials, we are obligated to publish our data and interpretations in reports so that others may benefit from our efforts.

After digging up sites, archaeologists are also obligated to curate the artifacts we find and the many records we generate. This means that we must pay to put them into museums where they will be properly stored so that they may be displayed and studied by others far into the future.

The goals of PAR are simple. We want to continue doing archaeological research in the West Pasture and in other places across the Texas Panhandle and Southern Plains, and we want to encourage the long-term protection of these irreplaceable resources. Our official slogan is "Investigating the Past to Inform the Future."

All of us involved with PAR believe that we have an obligation to inform the general public about what we are doing archaeologically and the exciting things we are learning. This book, funded through PAR and a generous grant from the David D. and Nona S. Payne Foundation of Pampa, Texas, is one small step in that direction.

Plains Archeological Research

Figure 25: Logo of the nonprofit group Plains Archeological Research.

You can find out about PAR on our website at www.plainsarch.org.

Conclusion

I view prehistoric sites on my ranch as a perishable record of people who lived here hundreds or thousands of years before I arrived. They weren't my blood kin, and I never knew them, but we belong to the same human family.

I respect those people and want to preserve the memory of their time on this piece of land. As far as we know, they didn't have a written language, so our only communication with them comes from the objects they left behind: houses, tools, weapons, pottery, food scraps, and mysterious items like the incised rib bone.

I am the custodian of that vault of information. It's an important job and I want to do it right.

John Erickson

Index

Note: Index entry numbers in italics refer to images.

Index

Index

Index

Index

Index

Index

Index

Index

Publication of this book was funded, in part, by a
grant from the
David D. and Nona S. Payne Foundation,
Pampa, Texas.

Printed in the USA
CPSIA information can be obtained
at www.ICGtesting.com
CBHW030209190524
8776CB00005B/652

9 781682 831229